One

Rides Alone

Bike and Hike
Uttarakhand

Ketan Joshi

INDEX

Prologue

I looked at Delzad in amazement!

I couldn't believe my ears! My eyes were saying that it was big and hairy and ugly enough to be Delzad, but my ears were saying that...

...DELZAD HAD ACTUALLY REFUSED TO COME FOR A RIDE!

WTF!

No no no no... I must be hearing things. This can't be. I blinked my eyes several times to clear them, wiggled my little fingers into my ears to clean them, and asked him again.

'BAWA! LET'S GO FOR A RIDE!'

And to my utter amazement, he repeated - 'NO!'

I reeled! I rolled! I rocked! I rattled!

The world must be coming to an end, with such a perversion of the natural order of things!

The Amigos were refusing to ride!

Firstly Adi had gone and fallen...er...fallen in love, I mean - and so it looked like his riding license was getting pulled. He would blush and hem and haw and run away when we talked about going on the next ride. Already he had run away early from two rides - 'Three men ride the cliffhanger' and 'Three men ride west' - and now he was a non-starter - scratched at the post! He was not available to ride at all… poor ex-rider…

It was like the three little pigs - the first little porker built his house out of straw and the big bad wolf came and huffed and puffed and blew his house down!

 And now - Delzad was also refusing to ride! What was going on?

Delzad flushed under my shocked gaze, and his face flashed red, orange and green like a malfunctioning traffic signal. His dense curly hair coiled and uncoiled like the fretful porpentine and he looked like an embarrassed large ex-rider…which he was!

'I can't help it!' he cried 'I would have loved to go - but I have to work! Work! Alas! Work! BOOHOOHOO…' he couldn't even cry out loud and curse his boss - because he was his own boss - he was self-employed!

The second little pig built his house out of …um…er…I don't remember - but something fragile I suppose. 'Coz the wolf came and blew him…er…blew his house down as well, with a few strategically placed huffs and puffs

I left him sobbing there, and walked home with leaden feet. How will I ride now?

SHE WHO MUST BE OBEYED saw my oval face (it was too fat to become a long face…) and asked what was up…or down, rather. When I told her that I was not going on a ride because the other two Amigos were not coming - she just flashed her eyes at me!

WHAT NONSENSE! HOW DOES IT MATTER IF YOU ARE ALONE?

Eh?

ARE YOU A MAN OR A MOUSE?

Eh?

GO AND RIDE, MAN! IF NO ONE COMES - RIDE ALONE!

As Rabindranath Tagore said - 'Ekla Chalo Re'.
 Never be afraid to walk alone. If no one accompanies you - then screw 'em - you walk your path alone!

What if I have a puncture? Breakdown? Lose my way? Get lonely? All these fears are pointless, and the worst things are handleable. Just have faith and go for it.

Screw it - Just Do it!
Ekla chalo re!
If no one walks along with you - Walk your path alone.

ONE MAN WILL RIDE ALONE!

Solo riding

This would not be my first solo ride - actually, my first rides were all solo rides.

My story of motorcycling was rather back-to-front. Most Indians start their vehicle driving life with a two-wheeler - they get a two-wheeler to go to college or when they start commuting to work, and later upgrade to a four-wheeler. For me, it was the other way round.

I was never into motorcycles as a teenager or young adult. Growing up in Mumbai, two-wheelers were never a part of our mind-space at all. Unlike other cities, Mumbai had a good quality, reasonably priced and dependable public transport system - and so we were happy travelling in buses, trains, autorickshaws and what not - and had no need of... or urge for ...a bike. The first vehicle I bought was a car - and was extremely happy in my little air-conditioned box, listening to music and being insulated from the noise and pollution of the dense city traffic.

Two-wheelers? Ha. That's for mugs!

In fact I can tell the actual day when I suddenly fell in love with motorcycling. It was on a backpacking trip in the Lahaul and Spiti valleys in Himachal, where me and Bharathi were traipsing across the place in state transport buses. We were staying in a hotel near the ancient Tabo monastery, and suddenly I see a flock (herd? Pride? Gaggle? Murder?) of Bullets parked outside.

* * *

Boy O boy! What an awesome sight!

It was the first time that I appreciated a Royal Enfield for the magnificent machine that it is, standing arrogantly on that mountain path and showing off its cool mods.

Holy cow! I said, and fell in lust. What wonderful things!

Later in that trip we hitched a ride from a group of firangs who were going to Dhankar, a monastery off the beaten track, and I think that was the first time I sat on an Enfield. And I was immediately hooked!

'Man, I gotta get one of these' I thought.

* * *

(I wrote about this episode in detail in my book 'One man goes on a bus - Spiti and Ladakh by public transport' Do check it out.)

But many years went by, and I didn't. Didn't get a bike, I mean. At first it was no mystery – I had no money, I didn't have a 2 wheeler driving license, I didn't know how to ride a bike, I didn't know any bulleteers. But then I joined a cool start-up company in Bangalore - and the place was full of Enfield riders! You couldn't throw a brick without braining a Bulleteer. But, the only thing I did was to letch at all the bulls I saw on the road, visit the website, go to the showroom, and talk in general terms to bull owners – without making the shift from being a bull letcher to bull owner.

God knows how long that phase would have lasted until Bharathi got sick of my moaning, and took things in hand by buying me a bike for my birthday - to be precise, she bought me a Royal Enfield Thunderbird Twinspark 350 cc. We took possession on the auspicious day of Ganesh Chaturthi, and the grinning showroom owner gave me the keys and invited me to ride my new steed.

'Alas, no' I said. 'I don't know how to ride one. Please deliver it to my house.'

The guy was utterly foxed!

And what he wanted to say was voiced by my brother later 'Are you nuts? You are going to learn to ride on a brand new Bullet? What's wrong with you?' he said, while mentally kicking himself for not having the dingle-dangles to buy a bull himself. (This was a common refrain. Everyone would come to me and ask why I am buying a bike so late in life, and after a few minutes say that they wished that they could buy a bike themselves and go for a ride somewhere)

Anyway, so now I had this bee-yoo-tiful black Thunderbird Twin Spark standing in my garage, knocking everybody's eye out. I then got myself a learner's license and started figuring out the clutch and accelerator and kick and how to avoid contact between my butt and the road. I rode around to town and to office and whatnot, but didn't graduate to longer rides. Somehow, I never got around to it. Basically, I didn't have the guts!

People I knew were riding to the Himalayas, and the beaches and to all kinds of exotic places, but here I was with a maximum ride of 40 kilometres.

Wimp.

I could feel my bike also getting disillusioned with me, like a bride with an impotent groom. She would look at me hopefully when I mounted her, and roar with passion when I tweaked her accelerator, but only to be disappointed when I stopped at the office 15 minutes later. It was like the brave prince marrying the beauty, but not being able to consummate the marriage!

A whole year passed like this, and my beauty's mood became as black as her engine oil, and she started to give me hints in the way she backfired while starting, and staining the garage floor with black waste.

But suddenly one day I sparked into life! Bharathi's Bengali friend came over from Calcutta, and told stories of his own Thunderbird. He was 20 years elder to me, and he had also bought his bike just a year before I did - but the doughty babumoshai was riding all over the place and had even done the dream ride of Manali to Leh with his fellow bongs - while I sat and cowered at home! He was very polite, but I could feel the disdain flowing out of him.

'But bhy don't you ride sir?' he asked me.

'Dada, meri phat ti hai' I surprised us both with a candid answer. 'I am scared'

'Sab ki phat ti hai beta' he said, and I am sure he would have added 'dar ke aage jeet hai', if it had not been already taken as a slogan by a faggotty piss-coloured soft drink. 'But you have to conquer your fear and go beyond it! Ride saar, Ride!' he said, patting me paternally on the back.

So.

* * *

Am I to me talked down by a bearded rossogulla eater?!!

NO, I SAY!

I muttered and fulminated...and finally it happened!

My friend, Vijay Makwana, the gyaani gujju, suddenly decided that our social lives needed a second wind, and asked me to come to Sulafest, a party to celebrate 10 years of Sula wines at Nasik. I agreed, unusually so – because I have become a lazy fellow – and bought second sitting tickets on Indian rail to go there. Avoid the traffic you see....roads are so unsafe. Wifey was very happy – the car-going heathen is converted to chris-train-ity.

But is frequently the case, the conversion is not complete. Heathen beliefs are still alive and kicking beneath the baptised exterior, and the night before the trip, I abruptly changed my mind about going by train. The thought of travelling to the railway station and going in that smelly second class compartment became intolerable - and I called Vijay said that we will go by car. Vijay recoiled at the idea of doing the trip in my now-ancient car, and said that he would take his car, and I should join them. I agreed – the roads are so tiring nowadays...better to share the pain of driving.

And that is where God took a hand!

Out of the blue, I suddenly decided that NO – I will not go in that car! I will go by bike!

Bharathi was rather bewildered by rapid change of plans - first train, then my car, then Vijay's car...and now bike!. But I guess the time had come! The larva of the rider had hatched from the pupae of intention - and was wriggling around energetically in my head. I was infected with the riding virus.

The next morning I dug out an old leather jacket, packed some clothes and zoomed off into the dawn!

WOO HOO.

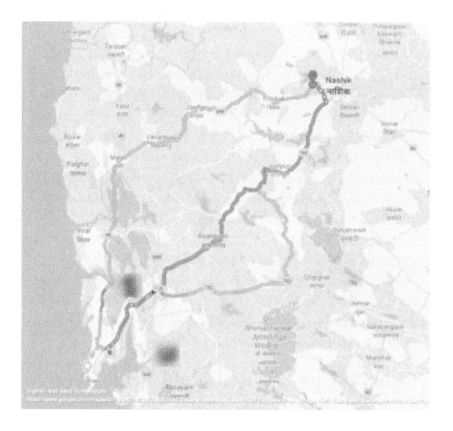

It was simply amazing to just put the bike into top gear and zoom down the road.

It was a beautiful ride on the Bombay Nasik expressway. I gave her the throttle and went to 60 - 70- 80 - 90. -100 kmph!

WOOHOO! I AM TALKING TO THE WIND, BABY!

I discovered that 100 kmph on a bike is very different from 100 kmph in a car. In car, you can hardly tell the difference…the only difference is the sound of the tyres, and the fact that the scenery is zooming by rather faster than usual.

But on a bike! It was totally different!

The bike is screaming and vibrating under you like a living thing…
The wind is screaming in your ears…
It tears at your face and eyes, and makes you tear up…
You can feel the grit and tar particles in the air…
The scenery becomes a blur…
The bike roars…
The vibration takes over your whole body…
You are one with your vehicle and the road and the atmosphere around you…

I learnt all kinds of new things about bike riding, and how it is different from car driving.

Like how when giant trucks pass you by, it really shakes you up! That giant blast of air as it displaces the air in front of it can actually throw you off the road!

And how you have to bend down and offer a low profile in the face of strong winds - or it feels like you are going to get blown right off!

And turning the bike at speed requires you to use your whole body and actually bend your bike at an angle!

* * *

You have to plan your braking in advance! The bike takes much longer to slow down than a car.

You can feel every cloud as it goes over you - the change of temperature and light.

You can feel the environment so much more keenly - the smell of hot tar, the coolness of a stream, the smell of cut grass, the earthy smell of the sugarcane in the truck in front of you...

I thought it would be my back which would cause trouble, but it turned out to be the ass which caused intolerable pain. After every two hours, I would be forced to stop and massage my aching buns. OW OW OW.

What a fun ride that was! My first ever solo ride!

As intense an experience as a virgins first kiss!

WOOHOO!

Immediately I could see a change in my Twinspark. She was sounding much better, and responding happily to commands. I could feel the happiness in her throaty roar, and when I got off, she swung her front wheel and tried to nuzzle me happily.

I was eager for the next ride now! I called Gurinder paaji - he was my colleague in Onmobile, and apparently a big bug in the biking world. He was a live wire with a local riding group called the Indithumpers - and later established a new group called the 'Bisons' - and was always eager to get new converts to the riding religion. In fact, it was he who came with me to the Royal Enfield showroom to buy the Twinspark.

* * *

Sure! He said happily, and invited me to join him for a ride to Lonar - an ancient meteorite crater about 500 km away. I gulped a bit. 500 km seemed a bit much...bloody hell, it's as much as Bombay – Goa! 'Don't worry dude' he said 'there's a couple of people coming along in a car, so if you get tired, then you can sit in the car, and one of those guys will ride your bike' .

OK, I said, let's give it a shot.

But to tell the truth, I was still scared!

It was like telling a still-bloody recent-ex-virgin that the next session would be BDSM, back door, golden showers and groups. A bit of a stretch. I was nervous.

And immediately I got an opportunity to wimp out.

I got invited to a college batchmates reunion that same weekend, where a bunch of old chums will meet up and have a fun weekend.

Ah! A Guilt-free reason to wimp out of the Lonar ride.

The guys had organised a bus and we all were going to pile on to that bus and have a jolly old picnic ride to the resort where we were going to hang out.

But that was when god stepped in. Again.

The Riding Virus reasserted itself!

No! I decided. I will not go in that blasted bus! I will ride down on my lovely loverly motorbike!

So I will ride after all – just change destinations from Lonar to Mahabaleshwar – 300 KM instead of 500. Sort of graduating from missionary to doggy, without going all the way to whips and chains.

And - more importantly - I will ride alone…and not as part of a group.

Bharathi is always most happy when one takes the adventurous option rather than the lame mainstream one and was like - GO FOR IT! She even advised me on the most fun way to get there - to take the ferry from Mumbai to Rewas and leave on Friday evening instead of Saturday morning.

I didn't even know that there was such a ferry! Wow! There's a ferry? Really? A ferry you can take a bike on?

SHE just rolled her eyes at me - and commanded me to pack my back and MOVE IT! MOVE IT! MOVE YOUR ASS! RIDE! RIDE! RIDE!

So, there I was, chasing the setting sun to the ferry wharf – the first time I laid eyes on the place. There used to be a big network of ferries from Bombay once, but now only two remain - One ferry across the bay to Alibag (Rewas jetty) and one ferry to Uran (Mora jetty). I would be taking the one to Rewas jetty.

(I gave a detailed history of the ferry system in my book 'Three Men Ride South - The Amigos ride to Coorg - check it out if would like to know more about it. Its very interesting)

* * *

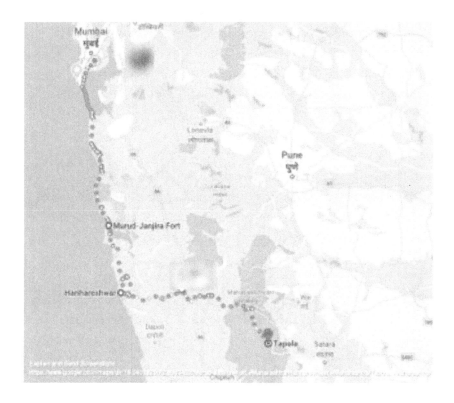

I was a bit nervous about loading the bike on the boat, but my fears (like most fears, I suppose) were unfounded. There were professional loaders who looked glumly at my heavy bike, and quietly and emotionlessly put it into the boat for a modest price. Charon could hardly have done better to his souls headed for the underworld. And with a lugubrious blow of the horn, we were off! It was a glorious feeling, sailing on that old ferry, looking at the setting sun and the towering expanse of Mumbai skyline and the salt breeze on my face. Absolutely wonderful.

On the boat there were 4 other bikers who also turned out to be bound for the Mahabaleshwar hills, so we had a chat about the route and stuff. They invited me to join them, but they were planning to do an overnight ride on the highway. I shuddered at the thought – doing it in daytime in a car itself can be daunting, what with lunatic truck drivers and stuff. And anyway, I had plans to fulfil an old ambition of mine – to do a motorcycle trip on the scenic coastal routes, on the calm and serene state highways, staying away from the blazing den of lunacy which is the National Highway.

But it was good to have them around, we chatted about this and that – they shared their experiences of driving to Mahabaleshwar - getting caught in torrential rains in the ghats at midnight, and other such jolly stories. Also, they had brought along some wine – which they companionably shared with me. So that was a good start!

We docked at the tiny wharf at a little town called Rewas just as it was getting dark, and having disembarked the vehicles, we set off into the darkness – they to catch the highway, and me to hit the coastal road.

It felt so good.

The experience of being alone on the bike on a completely dark road, with only the roar of the bike for company was amazing! I thought of riding with my visor up to feel the wind in my face, but quickly abandoned the idea after getting a face full of bugs. I rode on past Alibag, and had almost hit Revdanda bridge before I called it a night. It was dark, and apart from the safety issues, I was missing some fine scenery. Also, people go to bed early around these parts, and I didn't want to get stuck without accommodation for the night.

Having ignored all kinds of good hotels, I finally decided that I will stay in the very next hotel which comes, and it turned out to be a crummy dive with a room for Rs 150. But hey, promises are promises, so I stopped for the night, only popping out to buy some mosquito repellent. Having established my beachhead, I turned to religion – and had some deep discussions with a peg of Old Monk rum before I hit the sack.

I woke up at 6, had a cold cold brrr bath, and thus refreshed, hit the road just before first light.

That is the time to be on a bike!

It's cold and crisp, and the air is like wine.

Ah!

The views on that road are to die for – the sea on one side, and golden straw mountains on the other. I and Bharathi had done an impromptu trip here in the car back in 02 , and had discovered a wonderland. The coastal road goes past Alibag, Murud, and follows the bay of Murud to Dighi. But on a bike you don't need to do that – you can put your bike on the ferry from Agardanda and take the boat to Dighi. I am not saying that it's the best idea – because it's a bee- yoo- tiful drive on that road, but hey, I took the ferry just because I can. And the fact that I will do anything to get a new experience. The loaders rolled their eyes when they saw my big black one, and huffed and puffed and put it on the boat, and charged me an extra 20 bucks.

There were a bunch of Muslim dudes on that boat, looking really fine and dignified in white achkan and embroidered headgear. I wondered why they were dressed to the nines - and the coin dropped when I realised that it was Eid! Eid Mubarak all!

* * *

I gave one of them a ride till Diveagar, and he asked me if I was going to Harihareshwar. Well, I wasn't...but why not? Suddenly I had the urge to visit the ancient temple of Harihareshwar – it was one of Dad's unfulfilled wishes to go to Harihareshwar, so I thought I would make the trip there and do an obeisance in his memory. So off I went. The road was simply glorious, and I passed the turn off to NH17 as well, which was all to the good – saved me the trouble of asking people about it.

Harihareshwar is known as 'Dakshin Kashi', or 'Varanasi of the South' and is supposed to be the place where the Pandavas did their death ceremonies before setting off for the Himalayas, and it's a place with real character.

It's on a bleak mountain jutting into a bleak sea, surrounded by a sombre black sand beach. You are supposed to do a 'pradakshina' - a circumambulation of the rock. You have to climb down all the way to the shoreline and cross over the sharp and slippery rocks - which is possible only during low tide and in dry weather, else you are liable to get smashed to bits on that sharp and slippery rocky shore. I had come here before, but it was only on this trip that I was destined to complete that pradakshina. It felt really other-worldly out there - the dark and shiny rocks, the brown and menacing sea, the purgatory-like atmosphere...

I was suddenly and inexplicably overcome by emotion at one point and tears started flowing down my cheeks!

That moment was indescribable.

It was like a sudden emotional attack - a tidal wave of emotions crashing over me...with no provocation! I had not been sad or nostalgic or anything like that…it just happened. Can't explain it at all. I was sobbing like a child on that rocky shore, surrounded by that sombre atmosphere. Maybe it was the spirit of my father touching me.

Hareshwar was the family deity of the Peshwas, so it was well preserved over the years, but now the MTDC is trying to make it a tourist destination with bungalows and water sports and stuff – But I think it's a bad idea. It would be better to let that sombre place brood, and think of Shiva consorting with his army of bhoot and pisacha out there.

I did my obeisance, and booked a prayer ceremony - an 'abhishekha' in dads name and set out again.

I had a most emotional experience with the last 'Abhisekh' we had done. Our last trip as a family when dad was around was to our family deity temple at a place called Vyadeshwar, and we had booked an 'Abhishekh' there - and were told that it would be done as per its position in the line.

Oh.. Ok - we had said - and as time passed…we forgot about it completely.

Some months after that...Dad passed away suddenly! It was as sudden and unexpected as a lighting bolt - and the shock left us all shattered!

The 'Terava' - the thirteenth-day death ceremony for the liberation of the departed soul was going on at my house, and suddenly the postman came and rang the bell!
I was pissed – what a time for the postman to come! There is the death ceremony going on, the priest is chanting away, the

house is full of guests, and this dude comes and hands me a couple of envelopes. I took the envelopes and glanced at them - and was completely zapped! Shell shocked!

I was standing there frozen, holding those envelopes, desperately trying not to cry, when someone comes and asks me what has come. I showed him – it was the 'prasad' - the holy offering - from our abhishekh in Vyadeshwar!

What incredible timing, that stuff reaching home exactly on the day and time of the death ceremony!

Coincidence?

Perhaps.

The obeisance done, I was off again, crossing amazing ghats on my way to hit the NH17. The roads were really beautiful - and being on a bike rather than in an air-conditioned box, I felt it more more intensely.

I had decided that I will not stop till I hit the highway, and even after I hit the highway, it was so nice that I kept on going. I may curse the highway as being full of trucks and traffic, but if you want to put some miles, you are best off on the highway. Soon I was within striking distance of my destination.

I called my friends to check where they were and it turned out that they were still hours away!

Ah well - that was a good opportunity to sit and relax with a cold beer! Two or three cold ones later, I was in a much better mood and thoroughly enjoyed the short and scenic ride down to the resort.

* * *

We had an excellent time at the reunion, and on Monday it was time to head back. The ride back was uneventful – except for the fact that I had not slept much for the past 3 days, and I was really sleepy while negotiating the ghats. I went downhill in bottom gear at sedate pace – because I was a bit sleepy, and also the views were magnificent.

On the way down, one biker came beside me and tootled. I turned enquiringly, and was pleasantly surprised to see one of the guys from the ferry. They were also on their way back. I said that I will be taking the ferry, but he shook his head. Nopes, too late – the ferry will be over. Ride all the way back.

And so I did – 7 hours of continuous riding on the Bombay Goa road. I had to stop a couple of times when my ass was howling, but it was a smooth and eventless ride all the way home. After I crossed into Navi Mumbai, it had become fully dark and a beautiful ocean breeze had started. I put on some music on my ipod and rode the sea breeze home.

My back was sore, my butt was sore- but on the whole, I was in good shape. My black beauty was also happy, and was purring away to herself, like any well-ridden lady. 400 KM on the first weekend, and 600 KM on the second.

'All good things come in threes, I thought…let's see where the next ride takes me to.' was what I had written in my blog at the time - but interestingly, it was the last solo ride I did for a long time!

But it was the start of a whole new riding chapter.

* * *

My serious riding started some time later, when I went for the 'Tour of NH17' organised by Royal Enfield. The company had started these organised tours for nervous tyros like myself, where the Enfield company conducted the whole ride and hand-held the riders.

They planned out the itinerary, provided experienced ride leaders and mechanics and even a doctor! They had a truck to transport your luggage - and another empty truck to pick up any bike which might happen to die on the road! They booked the hotel rooms and told you where to stop for tea and so on - all you had to do was to sit on your bike and ride! This was an amazing experience, and left me full of enthusiasm to continue riding!

These conducted rides are a special feature of Royal Enfield, and they do a lot of these experiential marketing activities for riders. They started with conducting a ride to Leh, Ladakh - 'The Himalayan Odyssey' - and this was such a roaring success that they added a number of marquee rides all over the country. I would unreservedly recommend these rides as being the best way for a newbie to get into long distance riding.

This ride gave me confidence in doing long rides, and also introduced me to fellow bikers - including a certain Parsi gentleman called Delzad Karani.

Another fellow rider started a touring company - Konkan Moto tours - and we did a lot of riding with them for a couple of years - and I met another interesting bearded person in that group... Mr Aditya Dhurandar.

* * *

After a couple of years, KMT wound up - and me, Adi and Delzad formed our own little group - The Three Amigos! We went on a ride to Ladakh, just the three of us - 'Three Men on Motorcycles - The Amigos ride to Ladakh', and enjoyed it so much that we went on another ride the next year to Spiti valley - 'Three Men Ride Again - The Amigos ride to Spiti.'

* * *

My next solo ride was utterly unplanned!

* * *

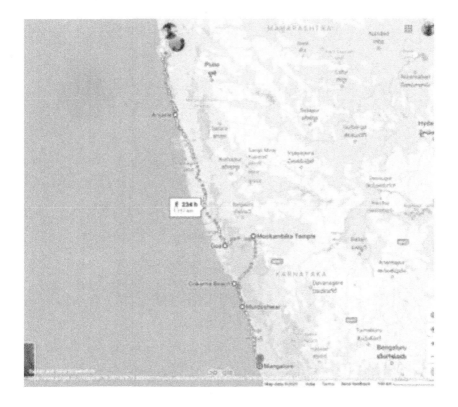

5 people - We three Amigos and two other friends - set out just for a weekend ride to Anjarle, a lovely village in the Konkan. I was so charmed by the ride, that when one friend - Rishi - suggested that we continue riding and go to Goa - I agreed!

I called Bharathi and told her that I would not be coming home after all - and she behaved in a particularly Bharathi fashion!

Instead of berating me for not coming home - she berated me for not going far enough!

'What will you do in Goa other than drink that same beer

and eat that same fish?' she demanded. 'Ride on further! Explore NH17! Go to Karnataka!'

'But…Rishi is not going on…' I whined. 'He is staying in Goa. I will be alone…'

'SO? BE A MAN! RIDE ALONE!'

Gee! Wow!

RIDE ALONE! WHAT A WONDERFUL IDEA! WOOHOO!

So I rode on alone - much to Rishi's amazement - and had a wonderful time! I explored the western ghats, the forests and the sea shore, and went to the coastal temple of Murdeshwar, the hidden backpacker haunts of Gokarna, the famous Krishna temple at Udipi and ended up in Mangalore!

My bike broke down in the middle of the forest, probably because I didn't go to visit Mookambika temple, and I had to flap around to get a truck and all - but that was amazing fun as well! It was also an example of my magnificent idiocy as well, where I managed feats of incredible stupidity! But the patron saint of Idiots helped me out, as he always does...

(Check out the whole story in 'Three Men Ride South - The Amigos ride to Coorg'. It is an amazingly fun story)

So that was the magical third solo ride - from Goa to Mangalore - and now I was a fully qualified to be a solo rider!

EKLA CHALO RE!

I SHALL RIDE ALONE!

Ride of Uttarakhand

After that awesome Tour of NH17 , I did a couple more rides with Royal Enfield - the Tour of Rajasthan and the Ride of Nepal.

But I was not a great fan of the RE rides nowadays - they are great for starting out, but can be a bit restrictive and regimented if you are used to doing your own thing.

But now that Adi and Delzad had abandoned me, I thought that I had no choice but to join an RE ride. And there was a great option coming up - a ride that I had not done before - the Royal Enfield Ride of Uttarakhand! WOOHOO! I had wanted to do a ride of Uttarakhand for a long time now, and this was a golden opportunity.

The Amigos had a new visiting member - Nitin. Delzad had bumped into him at the Royal Enfield service centre... Nitin had recently bought a Thunderbird 500 and was asking the service centre manager about how to go on rides. The manager must brightened up considerably on seeing Delzad - Aha, now I can can palm off this pesky customer onto another pesky customer! WooHoo! Then they can trouble each other and leave me alone! So he introduced them to each other - 'Delzad sir is a great rider...he keeps riding everywhere...you ...er...talk to him, OK?' and vanished into his office like an insect scurrying into its burrow.

Nitin must have been startled to see a big plug-ugly of a wooly-pated bawa in front of him...but then...Nitin is an engineer, so his whole life must have been full of the most awfully ugly people. Looking at bawa probably made him feel right at home. They started chatting and found that they were actually neighbours! They had factories next to each other!

The long and short of it (why long and short? Why not fat and thin?) was that Nitin also started riding with us and became a honorary or guest Amigo. We did a few rides to Goa together and had a good time. I found it soothing to have a guy older than me on the trip! What a change from these young twerps and hooligans and juvenile delinquents I have to hang out with normally!

'A mature mind at last!' I said to the hooligans
'An old-age home, more like' bawa muttered
'What was that?'
'Nothing…nothing…How's Jerry'
'Eh? Jerry? Jerry?' I was most puzzled 'Jerry who?'
'Mr Atrick.'
'Who?'
'Arre …Jerry Atric… HAHAHAHAHA'

Anyway - coming back to Ride of Uttarakhand… I called Nitin and told him 'Let's go for a ride! The Royal Enfield Ride of Uttarakhand is starting.'
'Arre…but I went for the Ride of Uttarakhand last year.'
'Eh?'
'What do you mean - eh? You only forced me to go!'
'I did?'
Oh yeah… I did. We were planning to go for the Kishtawar Killar ride (Three Men Ride the Cliffhanger) and Nitin wanted to come along. But I strongly suggested that he do a Royal

Enfield conducted ride first to get into the hang of doing a long ride. You get guides and mechanics and fellow riders and hotel bookings and all that stuff to make a hassle-free ride and is a good way to get used to long rides.

So we pushed him into the Ride of Uttarakhand and we set off for the Cliffhanger ride.

'So what? Do it again!'
'Eh? Again?'
'Why not?'
'But…'
'Do you want to ride or not?'
'Er…yes…'
'Will your wife let you go on a ride alone?'
'Er…no…'
'Will she let you go on a ride with me - just the two of us?'
'Er…no…'
'Then what choice do you have?'
'Er…you are ride…I mean, you are right! Even repeating a ride is better than no ride!'
'Exactly.'

And so, much to the astonishment of the Royal Enfield company - and Mrs Nitin - he booked himself for a repeat ride of Uttarakhand. It had been a wonderful ride experience, so he had no objections. And in fact, there were another couple of folks who were also repeating the ride.

We sent off the bikes to Dehradun by train - I knew the railway agent by name now and he greeted me cheerily! Where are you off to now? Oh, to Dehradun? Great! I will ensure your bikes reach without a hitch!

* * *

We were a beam of sunshine in his normal dreary life - the whiff of adventure perks everyone up! Most people are very happy to be involved in any small way in an adventure - and motorbiking trips are something that really appeal viscerally to most people.

We took a flight to Dehradun airport. It is actually midway between Dehradun and Haridwar/ Rishikesh - so you can take a flight there to go to either place. It used to be called the 'Jolly Grant airport' but now has been renamed as 'Dehradun airport'. It must have been a sheer toss-of-the-coin that decided between calling it Dehradun airport or Haridwar airport.

I wondered about the original name, which was really catchy - the 'Jolly Grant' airport. Was it named after a very jolly person named Grant? That would have been a cool story, but the truth seems to be more prosaic. The airport was developed in an area near 'Jauli' village. It was apparently a wooded area given

'On grant' to people to clear the forest and farm the land - hence it was known as 'Jauli Grant'. There are apparently other such names around - Arcadia Grant, Markham Grant, Karbari grant, Majri grant etc. The clerk who transliterated the name of the place into English wrote it as 'Jolly Grant' instead of 'Jauli Grant' - either he was really literal or tongue-in-cheek.

This must have been the only flat land around, so it was developed as an air strip. The legend goes that one elderly lady from a rich industrialist family wished to go on a pilgrimage to the 'Chaar Dhaam Yatra' before she died - and it was not possible for her to go in cars and trains and stuff - so the moneybags family acquired the land and built an airstrip or a helipad there.

A good story - but sounds a bit suspect to me, considering that a train goes right to Haridwar - but it makes for good reading.

What really helped the airport to come up was the Tehri dam. There was a huge dam project announced in Tehri Garhwal in the 70s- and this airport was developed to become a cargo hub to service that. The first passenger flights were started there by Vayudoot airways in the mid 70s. This could have been the beginning of big things - but the airport seemed to remain in stasis as a tiny one-plane town for years and years, till it was rediscovered and redeveloped during the airline revolution in the 2000s, to service the growing tourism sector and enable people to head into the hills with ease.

It is now quite a bustling little place, with daily flights from Mumbai and Delhi - and they have made a spanking shiny new building, all glittering with glass and chrome and steel. The government has done a good job of spiffing up the small airports in the country and a number of them are surprisingly fancy nowadays - Jaipur, Chandigarh, Dehradun, Pune, Nagpur, Ahmedabad, Lucknow etc. I remember them as being small and basic airports and now they are glittering and modern! India shining! Though of course, this meant that the airport fees have gone up significantly! But then you can't have everything - as the man said when his mother-in-law died, but they came down on him for the funeral expenses.

We took a taxi to the railway station and collected our bikes - a surprisingly efficient and swift affair - I was impressed! -We put on our panniers and filled up petrol and made our way to our hotel and checked in.

We were in Uttarakhand! WOOHOO!

Uttarakhand is a very new state - just a few years old. The area used to be a part of the state of Uttar Pradesh, and had been recently carved out from it to form a new state.

'Uttar Pradesh' literally means 'Northern region' and the name has no historical meaning whatsoever. In old times, the area used to be full of kingdoms and principalities of various sizes and importance - from the large states of Oudh (Awadh) and Agra to the small states like Rampur and Tehri-Garhwal to the really small ones in the Rohilkhand, Bundelkhand and Doab areas. When the British came and conquered them all, they did not think it worth dealing with each one separately - and so clubbed them all together into one administrative area. It was first called 'The United Provinces of Agra and Oudh', then renamed to just the 'United Provinces' - and was known by the short-form 'U.P.'

After independence, the government did not want to continue using the name 'United provinces'. For one thing it smacked of Raj memories which the country was trying to forget, and for another - there were no 'provinces', as all the princely states had been absorbed into the Indian union, and had been welded into a single state. But everyone was used to the short-form of 'U.P.' And so they decided to rename the 'United Provinces' to 'Uttar Pradesh' - it did not mean anything in particular, so no state could feel particularly slighted, and everyone could continue to call the place 'U.P.'

But the state was too damn big and had too many people. From a practical point of view, it was difficult to govern - and from a political point of view - if a party won the state of UP, it was as good as winning the whole of India - as they would have enough seats in Parliament to have a majority. Thus the decision was taken in 1998 to split the state into two parts and remove the hilly mountainous bit and make it a separate state. The new state was first called 'Uttaranchal' - but the locals protested that this is a damn silly name - and the state was renamed to 'Uttarakhand' on 1st Jan 2007.

This state consists of all the beautiful parts of UP! It is full of scenic mountains and forests and rivers and is chock-full of religious hotspots and pilgrimage points. They are very keen to attract as many tourists - and pilgrims - as possible and so call themselves the 'Devbhoomi' - or 'Land of the gods'. (This makes the neighbouring state of Himachal Pradesh very angry - as they also call themselves as 'Devbhoomi') They have all the good stuff in the tourism game - they have ample amounts of must-visit pilgrimage spots for the religious crowd, they have the venerable hill-stations like Dehradun, Mussoorie etc for the holiday crowd, they have Raj relics for the empire crowd, hiking trekking river rafting for the adventure crowd, the Yoga trail at Rishikesh and so on and so forth.

* * *

We were going to have a great time! The Ride of Uttarakhand would follow a very classic route.

Dehradun - Kausani - Munsiyari - Binsar - Corbett - Dehradun. I would leave the group at Binsar and head out for my solo ride!

* * *

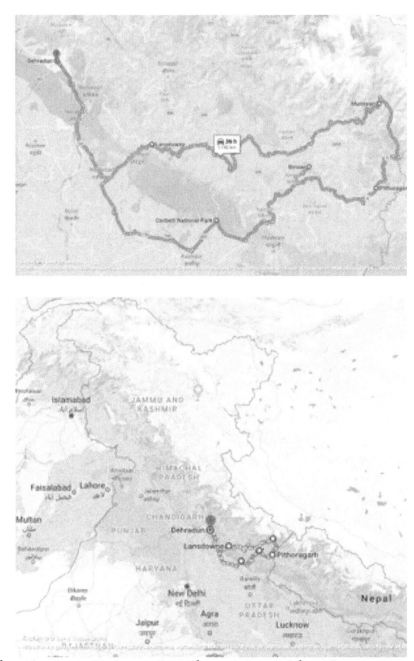

The ride was indeed great fun! The members of the ride were a nice bunch - there were people of all stripes - veteran riders, young turks, an aussie dude who's family had been running an orphanage in India for three generations, a couple of guys from Malaysia, a spouse of a nordic diplomat, a lady rider from the North East - and a few media guys.

They all looked at me rather disbelievingly when I told them that I write books about motorcycle touring. 'Really?' they seemed to be saying 'This fat loser is a tourer and writer? Really? Really?' - but they were very nice about it, and didn't say it to my face.

Most of them seemed to be alarmingly good riders too - far better than me! A lot of them were riding the Royal Enfield Himalayan - my first look at this bike in action - and they all seemed to effortlessly go over mud, stones, water etc - where I would huff and puff and look at them in wonder! It was only a year later, when I did my first ride on the Himalayan and discovered its magical powers, did I realise how they were doing it. But at the time I just felt like I was in the company of giants! Wow!

The most excitement we had was when a girl misjudged her handling of a turn on the road - and rode right off a cliff! There was no sign of any fall or slide or scratch on the road - and we might never have known what had become of her…except for the lucky chance that she was talking to her husband on a wireless connection, when she suddenly squeaked and got cut off! Imagine the poor guy's puzzlement when he couldn't find neither hide nor hair of her on the road! Had she been snatched to heaven on a flying horse or something?

'But they would hardly have taken the bike too…' another guy said.

Well - that was true. What would God do with a Royal Enfield?

So they hunted around - and finally found that she had skidded on a bend in the road and flown right off the cliff!

But it all ended well - amazingly well! The lady was unscratched! She fell not too far and in something soft, and managed to climb back up to the road - much to her husband's relief. The guys managed to pull her bike out of the cliff and both came safely to the hotel - and the girl was so brave that she continued on the ride - sitting behind her hubby as a pillion! Wonderful!

You can read an article and see a great video about the ride here- https://www.motoroids.com/features/royal-enfield-tour-of-uttarakhand-2018-and-how-i-returned-a-transformed-rider/ by a journalist dude who was along for the ride.

I told the RE team that I would be leaving them at Binsar and striking out on my own - and the lead organiser took it calmly - much to my relief. The last time me and Delzad had done this was in the Tour of Rajasthan and the organiser had gotten all het up about it and made us give him a letter of indemnity and whatnot. (And Delzad had immediately had an accident and broke his leg! Read about it in 'Three Men Ride Again - The Amigos ride to Spiti')

He made the announcement during the evening get-together and everybody clapped and wished me well - and quite a few guys looked very envious too!

Their ride was getting over - while mine was just starting!

WOOHOO!

* * *

On the morning of the first day, it was Ganesh Chaturthi - the first day of the Ganpati festival. As per mythology, it was the birthday - or creation day of my favourite deity Ganpati, the elephant-headed god of wisdom. I always had a loving relationship with this figure and looked at him as a good friend! Good ol' Ganesha - my old china… as a cockney might say.

The story of Ganesh Jayanti (Birthday of Ganesh) was - Like all ancient mythological stories, rather a gory story with a lot of deaths and blood and action!

The story goes that Shiva had gone out on a toot with his gang of misfits and reprobates - the 'gana's - and Parvati - his wife - was left all alone at home. She got very bored at home, and decided to create a child for her to play with. Being a goddess she didn't have to go through all the …er…um… process that we mere mortals have to go through. She just washed the mud off herself while taking a bath - formed that mud (or clay - if you want to be all classical) into the form of a little boy and breathed life into it…and hey presto! You have a child! (Don't spoil a good story by asking how much mud she had on her person and all those silly logical questions!)

The child was immediately most attached to his mama and they had a good time playing together all alone as his papa (Sort of?) was off on a trip with his 'Gana' chums ('Gana' could mean subjects or followers or companions…depends on the context)

When Shiva was due to come home, Parvati decided to go for a bath and get ready to receive him (and to probably break the news that he was a father to a bouncing not-baby boy) and so told the kid to guard the door and not let anyone come in till she was done.

Unfortunately for him, Shiva came back a bit early - and must have been understandably taken aback to see a kid standing guard outside his door.

'Hey kiddo! Who are you? What are you doing here?' he must have asked.

'I am Parvati's son.' He replied - and Shiva must have reeled and clutched his brow! How long had he been gone? What was going on here?

'Get out of the way! I want to talk to Parvati!'

'No! You can't go in!' the kid replied. 'I will kick butt of anyone who tries to enter!'

Shiva couldn't bring himself to shove the kid out of the way - so his chief Lieutenant, Nandi the bull, tried to shove him aside - and was utterly shocked when the little kid turned out to have superhuman powers and kicked him senseless! Seeing this, all the 'gana's attacked the kid - and there was a big melee and to-do and before you knew what was happening - everyone was dead! Every 'Gana' I mean - the kid was unscratched!

Shiva saw red! How dare this stripling kill his people? He lost it and attacked the kid with his trident - and obviously no one was strong enough to withstand the god of gods - and the kid's head was cut off and crushed!

'Oops' Shiva said, as his surge of rage subsided. 'What just happened? What's going on?'

And just then Parvati came out of the door - with probably a towel wrapped around her damp hair - and greeted her lord and master with a winning grin…which was replaced by sheer shock on seeing the carnage on her doorstep!

'Oh! You are back! How lovely! I wanted to show you….EEEEEEEEEEEK! YOU HAVE KILLED MY SON! YOU MONSTER!'

'I…er…' Shiva was speechless - utterly taken aback. Son?

What son? He had a son? And he had killed his son? WTF? What … what…

'HOWDAREYOUKILLMYBEAUTIFULBABY? FIRSTYOUGOOFFONTOOTSANDLEAVEMEALONE FOR DAYS AND NOWYOUHAVEKILLEDMYSON?! OOOOOOOOOOOOO'

'Here…here….relax…everything will be fine…' Shiva said hurriedly. 'Just calm down and tell me what's been going on here? Where did this son come from?'

'Oh?'
'Ah?'
'Hm.'
'I see.'
'Rather.'
'Umhmm…'

Once Shiva was up to date with what had happened - and probably got the earful of a lifetime - he said 'Don't worry… I will sort everything out…'

First he said 'All you lazy ganas… get up at once!'

'But they are dead!' Parvati cried.

'That's no excuse!' GET UP YOU LAZY LOT!' - and all of them were restored to life! They got up, looking all embarrassed at having been killed by a beardless stripling.

'Now you kid… BE ALIVE!'. But the kid would not move. Puzzled, Shiva went over to check.

'Oh… I see…I seem to have…er… crushed his head…'

'YOU CRUSHED MY BABY'S HEAD!'

'Yes yes…but don't worry…heh heh…Hey you lot - go to the forest and bring me the head of the first animal you see.'

'Which animal, boss?'

'JUST GO AND DO IT AND DON'T ASK SILLY QUESTIONS!' Shiva snapped, looking sideways at the fulminating Parvati.

'Yes boss, yes boss.' They hurriedly went off into the jungle - found an unfortunate elephant - chopped its head off - and brought it back.

'AN ELEPHANT! REALLY?' Shiva shouted, waving his hands about. 'SEE THE SIZE OF THE KID AND SEE THE SIZE OF AN ELEPHANT!'

'But…you said grab the first animal we come across…' they whined.

'Oh Dammit! This will have to do.' Shiva growled and put the elephant head on the kid and did some magical godly stuff - and hey presto…you have a kid with an elephants head! The poor kid must have had quite a shock when he realised that he had a very long nose and huge flappy ears and a taste for peanuts!

To make up for all the confusion, Shiva conferred a bunch of superpowers on him and made him the boss of all the 'Gana's.

'What's your name anyway?' he asked.

'I…er…'

'Never mind - now you will be known as the boss of all the gana - you are now 'Gana-pati' '

'Or Gana-esha' Parvati said. 'God of the all the Gana'

'I…er…OK… Ganapati or Ganesha…whatever works. You will be the remover of obstacles - Vighna-harta- and since we are at a new beginning here, you will be the God of New beginnings as well. Let all prayers, events and ceremonies start with a prayer to you.'

And so let us start my first solo ride with an invocation to

Ganapati - Vighnaharta - God of new beginnings and Remover of Obstacles.

Om Jai Ganapati!

Binsar to Kausani - via Mukteshwar

Well, the time had come for the obstacle-remover to do his stuff! I already had an obstacle!

I was packing up to start my brave solo ride - and I noticed that my riding gear was feeling a bit strange.

Riding gear are basically outer garments made of a stiff and strong material which will prevent you from having a nasty scrape if you take a toss off your bike and go sprawling on the tarmac.

And they are 'armoured'!

Which sounds very cool - like Sir Lancelot going off to fight the dragon or something - but is a just a rather 'martial' way of saying that they have special silicon-rubber pads stuffed inside them to protect impact points of the body - so you have the armour on your shoulders, elbows, back and on your knees.

I noticed that the armour was feeling a bit weird around the shoulders, so I opened up the jacket to take a look - and imagine my disgust when I saw that the armour piece was broken! The rubber must have hardened up due to sun and rain or just age - and had broken in two!

Shit! This was useless. It had zero protection value!

I looked at it in disgust - and then it struck me that the other shoulder pad was equally old! What kind of shape was it in? I fished it out...and it was broken too!

* * *

I looked at it in astonishment. I never had such a problem with my Indian-made Cramster jackets - but my fancy imported Australian Rjays was falling apart!

Then I checked my elbow pads - and they were broken too!

My pants were RJays as well! I looked at my knee pads...and well...you know where this is going.

I laid them all out on my bed and looked at them thoughtfully. Hmm.

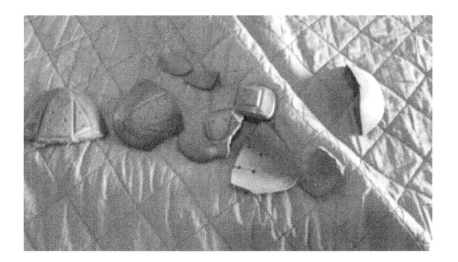

CE certified armour indeed. Gah! Double Gah!

Yo obstacle-remover god! Need some help here!

And I got it too!

I scurried around asking if anyone had any spare armour - and various kind people donated the spare armour they had. I mangled to snag one pair for the jacket and one pair for the pants! What a relief!

Thank you obstacle-remover!

I decided that elbows were more likely to get hurt in a fall rather than shoulders - so I put them there and hoped for the best. The ideal was not to fall at all of course - but having this stuff in gives you peace of mind.

Then it was time to face the second problem! My little water-heater had broken!

I am partial to my cup of tea - and get very cross with a bad cup of tea. And the sad truth is that one can never get a good cup of tea in a hotel. The staff is is rarely awake and active in the early morning when I want my cuppa - and even when they are, the variation in the quality is terrible.

Earlier, there was nothing to do but to grin and bear it… or to be more accurate, curse loudly and crib bitterly - but now there was a fantastic solution. Various Indian tea companies had come out a product of ready-to-make Indian-style tea mix … it is a mix of tea, sugar and milk powder and you just pour hot water into it to get an awesome cup of tea.

While this was great - it was valueless without a way to get boiling water on command - a proper roiling boil. But now you get little one-cup water heaters which can heat up a cup of water in minutes!

Put these two together - and you have a solution to all of life's problems!

With great foresight, I had packed a supply of tea sachets sufficient for the whole trip and a heater and even my own cup!

Unfortunately, my heater got broken just yesterday and stopped working! What a problem! I was heart-broken! No tea? NO TEA? OH NO!

'Don't worry re.' Nitin consoled me, all the engineer in him coming out. 'We will get it repaired, never fear.'

It was strange that I was so worked up about a dinky little water heater - and not so much about my bike!

My chain had been making funny noises for few days - and had even packed up during the ride! The bike had stopped dead in the middle of the road, and I had to wait for the 'gun wagon' -

the repair van with the mechanic and the tools and stuff to come and fix me up. I was very worried about it and told the mechanic to spare no effort in getting the problem solved, and change any parts if required... but the blighter coolly told me that there was no problem...the chain was just a bit loose, that's all. He did something to it and it seemed to be working - but I was still worried about it.

'You know I am going on a solo ride.' I said. 'I will be all alone.'

'Yes saar.' He said, nodding his head intelligently.

'So are you sure that this chain will present no problems?'

'No saar. No problem! I fix!'

'You dont want to change the chain and sprocket set, to be on the safe side?'

'No saar - Don't worry! I fix!' he beamed a thousand watt smile at me.

I looked at him doubtfully. I had interacted with Royal Enfield mechanics too many times to share his confidence. I went and buttonholed Rohan, the ride leader.

'Hey Man - are you sure that the chain will cause no problems?'

'What's the mechanic saying?'

'He is saying that there will be no problem.'

'Then it's OK!' he cried. 'A Royal Enfield mechanic has spoken!'

I looked at him doubtfully - but allowed myself to be carried away by the confidence of these two Royal Enfield personnel. Big mistake!

After all - the Obstacle-Remover was on my side!

And the Patron Saint of Idiots!

* * *

We all finally geared up and left the hotel - We would ride together till the main road and then I would take the high road and they would take the low road, so to speak. Me and Nitin left together - with Nitin keeping an eagle-eye out for a repair shop. He suddenly spied the tell-tale spiral of a soldering-iron holder in one shop and we went in there to get that little heater fixed.

The shop guy examined it with the keen eye of the artisan and got to work to repair it. When he was almost done, he casually asked 'How much did you buy this for?'

'Oh - about 40 rupees I think.' I replied

'Ah well... you won't get it for so cheap here.'

'I won't get it for so cheap here...you mean you have a heater like this to sell?'

'Yes sir.' He replied and pulled out a piece. 'But this is more expensive - this is a hundred and thirty rupees.'

I looked at the heater - and looked at the shopkeeper in wonder.

'If you had this to sell...' I asked 'Why on earth didn't you tell me that before doing so much effort to repair this thing?'

'Well - you didn't ask for a new one...you just asked for this to be repaired.'

I bought the new one, of course - and the fellow refused to take any money for the repair of the old one! 'Always better to have two rather than one, saar...' he said with a smile. 'And it was my fault for not telling you about me having one to sell. So no charge for repair.' These small town shops are something else! What a nice chap!

We made our way down to the main road and saw that one of our riders was standing there, waiting for us.

'Were you waiting here just to say good bye to me?' I said, feeling touched.

'No, not at all. Actually the rest of the guys got lost and have not come down yet. I am waiting for them.' He replied - then hastily added 'Er…I mean - I am also waiting for them…I was also waiting to say goodbye to you…hehheh…er…hrmmm'

We waited there and all the lost lambs finally found their baa-baa way down to the main road and I duly said bye and share man-hugs and back-pats with all of them. Finally all of them went off and Nitin also shook hands with me and said Good bye and rode off.

I was left there all alone.

Solo rider.

With suspect riding gear. And a dodgy chain.

Life couldn't be better!

WOOHOO!

I wandered lonely as a cloud
That floats on high o'er vales and hills!

Though obviously, this cloud was more of a guided cloud than one of those free-floating ones. I had gotten specific directions from SHE WHO MUST BE OBEYED. I was not to tarry and look at 'A host, of golden daffodils…' but should move my arse and make my way to Mukteshwar. Then, having seen that and ticked it off my list - I was to turn around and make my way to Kausani!

* * *

'What is there at Mukteshwar?' I asked

'YOU DARE TO QUESTION ME?' she roared, and I quailed, turning yellow as a daffodil.

'No no…' I stammered. 'I merely asked…'

'JUST MAKE YOUR WAY THERE ASAP!' she roared again and I shook like the daffodils 'Fluttering and dancing in the breeze.'

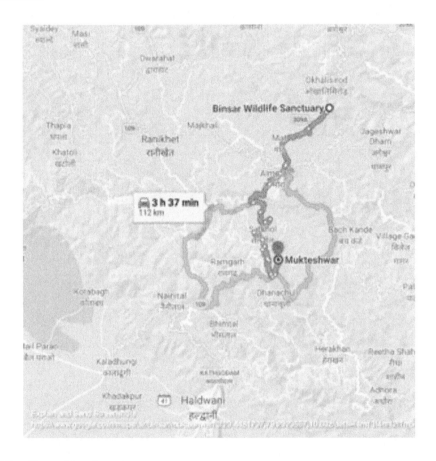

The Open Road

Out of the city and over the hill,
Into the spaces where Time stands still,
Under the tall trees, touching old wood,

Taking the way where warriors once stood;
Crossing the little bridge, losing my way,
Finding a friendly place where I could stay.
Those were the days, friend, when we were strong
And strode down the road to an old marching song,
When the dew on the grass was fresh every morn,
And we woke to the call of the ring-dove at dawn.
The years have gone by, and sometimes I falter,
But still I set out for a stroll or a saunter,
For the wind is as fresh as it was in our youth,
And the peach and the pear still the sweetest of fruit.
So cast away care and come roaming with me,
And know what it is to be perfectly free.

—Ruskin Bond

I immediately set out for Mukteshwar, and the scenery was
wonderful. This was the green Himalayas - unlike the brown
and stern landscapes of Ladakh and Spiti - and was wonderful
to see. There was hardly any traffic and it was just and the
thump thump thump of my Thunderbird on the road. I rode for
hours and hours, soaking in that view - the mountains, the trees,
the blue sky, the scudding clouds…

What perfect solitude!

In fact, there was nobody on the road at all.

Hmm.

This was too much of a good thing. Why wasn't there
anybody on the road? As per my calculations, I should be pretty
near Mukteshwar by now, and it was a famous tourist
destination…there should be quite a few cars about. But there
was no one! Nothing at all.

* * *

I checked the map on my phone - and uh oh…there was no signal! It was just showing a blue dot on a blank screen. Even the downloaded map was not showing up. Gah - it was technology up to its tricks again… I could just imagine the imp in the phone giggling to itself.

I finally saw a vehicle on the road and frantically waved it down and asked him if I was on the right road to Mukteshwar.

'Oh no no…bless you sir…you are far off your route…' he replied, chuckling.

'Oh really? Where does this road go?' I asked

'Oh this road goes nowhere…just a few farms and orchards and a lot of nothing. You need to turn around and ride for miles and miles and then take a turn…'

Hmm. This was an auspicious start to the ride I must say. Got lost straight away!

But then, the fatted calf is killed only when the prodigal returns - I am sure the good chap who did not stray didn't get any fatted calf chopped for him. It's good to be the prodigal… and stray… and return, of course!

I turned the bike around and went back to the fork in the road - and saw with some irritation that the path to Mukteshwar was clearly marked! I had just not noticed it!

Two roads diverged in a wood, and I—
I took the one less traveled by … and got hopelessly lost!
And found that it was the wrong way!
And so had to come back and take the one more travelled by!

- Robert De-frost

I finally made my way to Mukteshwar - and was quite taken aback by how busy it was! By sheer chance I had come by some lonely and beautiful back roads to my destination - and had a most beautiful ride!

So the road less taken was a good decision, after all! How strange.

Perhaps that's the secret of life - take the road less travelled by - but still keep an eye out for your destination.

Mukteshwar is famous for an old Shiva temple - where he is worshipped as the one who give you 'Mukti' - frees you from the endless circle of life and death. It is not that old as Indian temples go - being about 350 years old. A mere stripling, compared to the venerable old ones.
(But still older than the USA)

It was also famous for being the haunt of the famous Jim Corbett - the tiger hunter and conservationist. Unlike the cretins who kill animals for fun, Corbett only used to kill man-eaters. (Or at least, that's what he says in his books) He started out as a hunter who kills for sport - but then realised the damage that hunting had caused to the environment, and became a nature conservationist. He still killed tigers - but only if they became dangerous man-eaters due to injury or inability to hunt for any reason.
'Carpet sahib'- as he was affectionately called by the locals - was frequently called upon by the Government administration to kill man-eating tigers and leopards that were preying on people in the nearby villages of the Kumaon-Garhwal Regions.

He wrote books like ' Man-Eaters of Kumaon',' Jungle Lore' etc , and was also one of the first wildlife photographers of India and spoke out for the need to protect India's wildlife from extinction. India's most famous tiger sanctuary - the Jim Corbett National Park - is named after him.

Corbett actually hunted a man-eating tigress who had killed 24 people - in Mukteshwar itself! How cool is that.

He went out after the tigress alone and on foot - he walked all the way from his house at Nainital - 60 km on foot! - tracked her and shot her within 72 hours of his leaving home and returned back on foot! He wrote about this adventure in the book 'The Temple Tiger and More Man-Eaters of Kumaon.'

Apart from Corbett, another international personality to come here was the Nobel Prize winning scientist Robert Koch, who studied the terrible 'Cattle plague' here and started the IVRI - the Indian Veterinary Research Institute - at this location. The IVRI has now been relocated to the bigger town of Izatnagar, but the original facilities are still maintained as the IVRI research centre and the microscope used by Koch and other historical articles are kept in a little museum. A hill-carved 'cold room' once used to store biological materials- in those days before refrigeration - is now a tourist attraction.

It was pretty late by the time I reached Mukteshwar temple, and I was starved! I parked my bike and was immediately approached by a guide who offered to take me around.

'No thanks.' I said 'I am good.'

'Please sir…' he said. 'I have had no business at all today…'

Poor guy. I felt sorry for him. The guide fees was not much for me, but it would be a big thing for him. Maybe he was just playing me - but hey, maybe he wasn't!

'OK sure' I said 'But let me have a bite first.' I had a simple and tasty meal of piping hot Rajma and rice from a roadside vendor and then went for the guided tour. He took me around the temple through some pleasant forested trails and showed me the sights - an old ruined bungalow called 'Victoria house' and a rock with a hole in it called 'chauli jaali' - women desirous of a child are supposed to stick their head inside it to conceive (wouldn't sticking a more appropriate body part be more fun?). Next to it was the 'Adventure activity' - Zip lining - where you tie a carabiner to yourself and slide very fast down a long rope. I looked at it most suspiciously…it seemed to be a rather old and undependable looking rope to do zip lining on - especially for a super heavy-weight person like me.

'It's very easy sir…' he told me. 'A snap!'

Hrmpf!

There was a big stone there - with generations of people having carved their names on it. What is with this urge to write your names on walls? People have been doing it since untold generations … must be an urge to get a small bit of immortality, I suppose. 'Rajesh loves Meena' will live forever!

Apart from helping the local people, there is no point in taking that silly guided tour - you can just walk around by yourself. The temple itself was not particularly inspiring either - but the views were nice. The guide salaamed me there and walked off with his fee, hoping to snag another sucker before end of day, and I had a local drink made of rhododendron flowers - A local specialty!

Well - so much for Mukteshwar. It must have been a pleasant and sleepy place once, but now was a bit over-developed for my taste. And anyway I had a schedule to keep - I couldn't afford to hang out here.

* * *

I got on the bike and headed towards Kausani. I took the right road this time - and was amazed as to how quickly I was back on the main road! Wow - I had taken a really circuitous route to come here - not that I regret it in the least! It had been an inspired mistake. I had seen such lovely roads because of that!

Two roads diverged in a wood, and I—
I took the one less traveled by,
And that has made all the difference.

Maybe Robert Frost was just as much of a direction-challenged klutz as me!

The ride to Kausani was beautiful and - luckily perhaps - fairly uneventful, but it became dark and it was quite late by the time I got there. I stopped in the village centre, wondering where to find a hotel…but a hotel agent came running to me and asked me to check out his hotel.
Well - why not? Any hotel was fine, and this hardworking fellow would get his commission.

The hotel turned out to be quite nice - and it seemed that I was the only guest in the hotel! It was like the whole hotel was my private domain! I had a refreshing hot bath and a very tasty chicken dinner! I was clearly a winner-winner!

The first day of the solo ride had been most satisfying!

Mukteshwar and Kausani - and a glimpse of the 'Obstacle-remover' at work!

one man rides alone

Kausani to Joshimath

Woke up in the morning to this view!

Whoa!

If the visibility had been better, I could have made out the peaks of Trisul, Nanda Devi and Panchchuli - you apparently get a 300 km vista from here. But the rolling cloud banks had their own appeal - it looks like the mountains were floating in a magical space!

Kausani is a beautiful place, though it does not have any particularly famous place within it - there is Anashakti ashram where Gandhiji stayed for a few days and the ancient 1000-year-old Baijnath temple nearby. It would be a good place to just chill out and do nothing.

I had a nice cup of tea in the early morning (my famous heater and tea powder combo at work! HA!) and enjoyed the views.

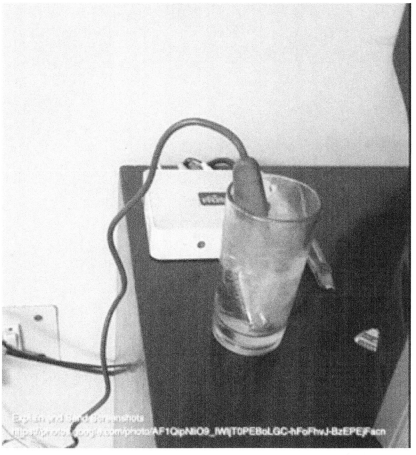

Today I would be going up north to Joshimath! Aha - Joshi is off to Joshimath!

* * *

After my long and tiring ride yesterday, I was determined to pace myself and stop every 30 km. For one thing it would reduce tiredness, and secondly - it would ensure that I dont fall into 'road hypnosis' or 'ride mania', and force me to look around and enjoy the views and vistas. Many times bikers fall into this urge to complete the ride as soon as possible and beat all records of time and distance - and forget that they are doing the ride not to prove anything to anybody - but just for the experience and pleasure of it.

And it would also remind me that 200 km is a respectable distance in mountain roads, and I should not take it lightly.

As I started riding, I realised that I had taken an excellent decision to stay in Kausani for the night. Yesterday I had been thinking about pressing on to Gwaldam - but now I could see that the roads were narrow and quite empty of habitation! And there was no great hotel infrastructure at Gwaldam and I might have got stuck! It is always a good idea to stop your ride before nightfall - nothing good happens on highways at night… especially for two-wheelers.

And after Gwaldam the roads were insanely screwed! The whole place looked like the aftermath of a vicious landslide! The roads were covered with slippery mud and streams of water and were a torture to ride on!

What the hell? What was all this? Had there been some major earth-quake that I had missed? What had caused such a major land slide?

I rode on bemusedly for miles and miles - and the roads were all like that. Dust, mud, muddy water, heavy traffic…it was like an endurance test. I could see hordes and hordes of trucks and motorised equipment chipping away at the mountains, and I wondered what natural calamity had happened here? The road was terrible. It was like a long continuous man-made landslide! I thought that Mumbai roads were bad…spare a thought for the locals here who would be dealing with this everyday!

I fought my way to Karnaprayag - and found that Karnaprayag town was also crowded and disgusting. Oh no! I rode out of there as quickly as I could. The problem was that most hotels and restaurants are concentrated in the midst of town near the bus stands and taxi stands - but I am sure that I would find something somewhere. There was no point in staying that crowded hellhole.

* * *

But as soon as I left Karnaprayag town, everything improved. The crowds and mess receded into the background and the roads instantly became bigger and better as I entered NH 7. I kept looking out for a hotel with a view of the prayag and finally I found one.

When I went in and greeted the owner and requested a meal - I saw a very welcome thing... a bed! The cheap dhabas on the highways used to have a bunch of 'charpai's - string beds - for the benefit of tired truck drivers who could stretch out and catch 40 winks - but this was the first time that I had seen one in a slightly upscale place like this.

'Can I use the bed?' I asked and happily took off my shoes and stretched out and went 'aaaah' as I relaxed on the bed. What a wonderful thing. I relaxed after that ghastly muddy ride and actually fell asleep for a few minutes before the waiter woke me up and told me that my meal was ready.

I enjoyed that simple vegetarian piping-hot meal - ah, what a pleasure! A most wholesome spread of vegetables, daal, rice, salad and freshly made chapatis. I do love a hot meal.

The hotelier was happy to see me enjoy the bed and the meal and beamed at me and we struck up a conversation.

'Why is the road so bad?' I asked. 'It was a bloody torture. Has been some natural disaster?'

'No no, no disaster. The roads are being widened! They are cutting the hills and that is causing the mud and water and general misery on the road' he told me happily. 'Modiji is doing work!' he said, referring to our new(ish) Prime minister.

This was the Rs 12,000 crore 'Char Dham highway' project!

The proposed highway will complement the under-construction 'Char Dham Railway' by connecting the four holy places in Uttarakhand states namely Badrinath, Kedarnath, Gangotri and Yamunotri. The project includes 900 km national highways which will connect the whole of Uttarakhand state.

The 'Char Dham railway' is also a huge project, with a budget of Rs 43000 crores! -these are Indian Railways's upcoming twin railway lines - from the existing Doiwala railway station near Dehradun to Gangotri and Yamunotri via a fork at Uttarkashi and another set of twin rail links from the upcoming railway station at Karnaprayag to Kedarnath and Badrinath via a fork at Saikot.

After the Konkan Railway and Jammu–Baramulla line, this line will be the most challenging railway project in Indian Railways due to high mountains, a large number of tunnels and high bridges and severe cold weather in flood, landslide and earthquake prone high altitude mountainous areas.

I grunted rather doubtfully at this.

While I am sure it is great to have good roads and railways, but the easy access will definitely destroy the beauty of the place completely. And may lead to terrible environmental disasters. We already had one of the worst disasters in Indian history when a long cloudburst led to the terrible Uttarakhand floods of 2013.

* * *

The Himalayas are pretty fragile mountains - as they are not volcanic in origin. They are basically giant ripples of mud - thrown up when the landmass of India rammed into the continent of Asia. While they are huge and grand - it doesn't take much to bring them down. They are held together by the binding force of dried mud and tree roots - and when humans cut down the trees and destabilise the mud - they can come crashing down.

Exactly this happened in 2013 when heavy rainfall triggered

off massive landslides - the rockfall dammed the rivers, which resulted in massive flooding and even more landslides. The tourism and property boom had led to huge unplanned construction - and this all collapsed to form one of largest natural disasters in India after the 2004 Tsunami. 3,00,000 people were stranded and starved and suffered before they could be evacuated and over 6000 people died - as per official records. The actual number could be much higher.

This was a pretty recent occurrence - but seemed to have been forgotten already! The government was cutting trees and drilling the mountains with even more frenzy... let's hope that there has been more planning this time round.

'So what do you do?' the owner asked politely. In India it is most impolite to not ask details of your life - what do you do, how much do you earn, are you married, how many kids etc.

I rather incautiously mentioned that I was a travel writer - and the hotelier responded like he was pricked by a needle! All the marketeer in him jumped out!

'Oh! You are a travel writer! Then you must write about my hotel... let me show it you!' he sprang out of his chair and dragged me upstairs.

'I am not that kind of writer...' I tried to wiggle out of it, but it was no use. He determinedly showed me all his rooms and showed me his terrace and what a fine view there was of Karnaprayag from there and how it was better than the view of the other rascally hoteliers, and so on.

It was actually quite a nice view of the confluence - and I hung around there to soak it in.

A 'prayag' means a confluence of two rivers - in this case, it was the confluence of the Alaknanda and Pindar rivers - which merge to form the Alaknanda, a tributary of the Ganges. Karnaprayag is one the five main 'prayag's of the Ganga - along with Vishnuprayag, Nandaprayag, Rudraprayag, Devprayag.

This prayag is called 'Karna prayag' because it is associated with 'Karna' - the most tragic figure in the great Indian epic - the 'Mahabharata'. The story of the Mahabharata is pretty complicated and gruesome - but the relevant part here is that there was a princess called Kunti, who prayed to the gods and was awarded a boon that she could call upon 6 gods to impregnate her and give her children!

'Really?' she said 'Are you sure this works?'

'Works? Works?' the boon giver replied in an insulted tone. 'Of course it works! Just say this mantra and the relevant god will appear and ...er....impregnate you!'

'Impregnate...but...without actually...er...'

'Bah! Remember - this is just a story! Read it as you wish!'

Kunti was like a kid with a new toy - she was actually a kid - she was just a teenager. She was still curious whether it actually works or not - and rather incautiously...said the mantra out loud! And there was a flash and a bang - BOOM - and the Sun God - Surya - stood there in all his glory!

'Awesome! I knew you couldn't wait!' he must have said. 'Off with those clothes! Let's get on with it!'

'EEEEK! WHO ARE YOU?'

'What do mean 'who are you'? I am Surya, the Sun God. You just called me here to impregnate you.'

'BUT I DIDNT MEAN IT!'

'That's too bad. I am here. Spread'em.'

'BUT I CAN'T HAVE A CHILD! I AM NOT YET MARRIED!'

'That's your problem, not mine.'

* * *

And Kunti had a bouncing baby! He was a magical baby - Shining and handsome - and he was born with magical ear-rings and armour and whatnot!

But he was a bastard child! And Kunti didn't want a bastard - not even a demi-god bastard! And she didn't want anyone to know that she had an 'illegitimate' kid - So she chucked the baby into a river and forgot all about him.

That's pretty cold. Patriarchy, and all that.
Better to kill the baby than admit to Pre-Marital…er… blessings…mantras…

But, like Moses - the baby didn't die - he floated on the river and was found by a poor driver (A charioteer, actually - but that's just an old-timey word for a chauffeur - or a 'driver' as we call them in India.) The driver was childless - and so was overjoyed to find a kid by sheer coincidence and raised him as his own son.

Kunti then got married to a prince of Hastinapur - Pandu. Unfortunately Pandu was impotent - due to a birth defect caused by his mom going pale with shock at the …er… shocking…sight of the person who was about to impregnate her (long story… very fascinating story, won't attempt to tell it here - but do read the Mahabharata if you have not already)
And also due to a curse from a sage - Rishi Kindama- , whom he - Pandu - shot while he - the sage - was making love! (Pronouns are the devil, aren't they?) It wasn't even Pandu's fault, he had no intention of shooting any sages - whether mediating or making out… but what happened was that the rather shy (and weirdly kinky) sage had turned himself and his

wife into deer (!) and were rutting away happily in the forest. Pandu was out hunting and saw the rutting deer and shot it - and must have shat in shock when the deer suddenly turned into a very angry - and nude - sage!

'But ...but... how was I to know that the deer was not a deer, but was a seer ... Oh dear...' Pandu protested.

'That is no excuse!' Kindama rishi growled. 'You should not shoot anyone or anything mid-hump! I curse you! The next time you try to get it on, you will DIE! AAARGGHH!'

The long and short of it was that he - Pandu - was warned that if he - Pandu- tried to get it on with any woman ever again, he - Pandu - would instantly pop off. No jiggy-jiggy for you chum - ever!

But then, what to do about the succession? Pandu's brother - Dhritarashtra - also had his own health problems - he was blind, and presumably impotent as well.

* * *

Who will inherit the throne? Where will the children come from?

But the wives of both brothers found their own different solutions - Kunti obviously had her magic wishes… she could call the gods to …er…do the deed and impregnate her. She had 5 coupons left - and she generously shared two of them with her co-wife, Pandu's second wife - Madri. (Poor Pandu - two wives, and not allowed to touch either!) - and between them they had 5 demi-godly - and legal! - children. These 5 half-brothers came to be known as the 'Pandavas' - the children of Pandu.

(Rather ironic that…considering that they weren't actually Pandu's children - but of various divine 'helpers'.)

Blind Dhritarashtra and his wife Gandhari went in for test-tube babies! Obviously they didn't have test-tubes in those days - so they used magical pots. No, really! As per the legend, the kids were grown in pots. They used a 100 pots - probably thinking that only a few would be viable…and imagine their surprise when all 100 worked! So Dhritarashtra and Gandhari suddenly had a 100 kids! And these were called the 'Kauravas' - the sons of the Kuru dynasty.

So now you have 5 kids from one bro and a hundred kids from the other bro - it doesn't take a genius to guess that you are going to have a doozy of a succession battle coming up.

'WE ARE THE TRUE KINGS!' the Pandavas roared.
'NO! WE ARE THE TRUE KINGS!' the Kauravas roared!
And they went to war.

And what of our hero - Karna - eldest son of Kunti, and the

one who was actually the true king?

Well - inspite of being the eldest, and the most accomplished warrior of them all, and having magical ornaments and armour and being handsome and kingly and legendarily charitable and good person - he could never break free of the stigma of being a lowly driver's son and was laughed at by both groups.

Kunti recognised him immediately - but never had the guts to accept him and give him his due - as this would expose her status as an ex-unwed mother!

He was cynically used by the leader of the Kauravas - Duryodhana - to fight against the Pandavas. Karna himself went all Anakin Skywalker and went over to the dark side and became as feared an enforcer as Darth Vader himself. He killed the sons of Arjuna and Bheema in battle - and was duly killed in his turn by Arjuna, as an act of revenge. (It's a very long story, with a lot of episodes.)

The story of Karna is a searing indictment of the class and caste system and of Patriarchy and cruel social mores, and he is a most 'Greek tragedy' figure - having divine powers, but full of flaws and cursed by misfortune.

Ended up committing Nepoticide and dying of Fratricide! Unloved and Unaccepted. Poor guy.

Karna is supposed to have meditated at this spot in Karnaprayag to attain or activate his super-powers - and is supposed to have been cremated here by Krishna, the divine avatar of Lord Vishnu.

* * *

Krishna was the only person who knew the whole story and had a lot of sympathy for him .

As he lay dying, Karna asked Krishna to take his body away from this accursed war zone, and cremate him at some virgin spot away from all this horror - and so Krishna brought his body all the way from the battlefield of Panipat in Haryana to the hidden confluence of Karnaprayag for the last rites.

This sombre story went through my mind as I gazed at the confluence. Poor guy.

I finally left the hotel and set out towards Joshimath. The road immediately became much better - it was a two- lane national highway, so it was comfortable and peaceful to ride on, and I had left the construction activity behind as well. It was a steep climb up to Joshimath and I was enjoying the twists and turns of the road, the bracing weather and the beautiful views.

In fact, the views were so tempting that I couldn't stop myself - and I stopped (sounds very Zen!) I parked the bike and went off to admire the views of the valley and the Alaknanda flowing below. While I was standing there, I was hailed by a couple of itinerant sadhus in the obligatory ochre robes and ash-streaked visage.

'Jai Bholenath.' I said.

'Jai Badri Vishal' they responded, and asked for alms and I smiled and gave them some money. The formalities completed, they stood around for a bit and chatted. They told me that they were walking from Badrinath to Kedarnath and then to Haridwar.

'Wow! That's a long walk!' I said.

'Nah.' They replied. 'All in a day's work…that's all we do - walk from one shrine to another. God's will is with us'

And indeed, they looked quite happy and healthy. They had nothing at all - but they seemed content with their lot. They bummed some smokes from me and we parted on good terms. As I turned away, I wondered who they must have been before they became sadhus - were they born poor and landless, or did they turn away from a rich life? Were they uneducated or educated ? Were they solo operators, or part of a group or cult or 'akhara'? But whatever they were, they seemed OK with it.

I got back on my bike and started riding up - and as I was riding, I passed a rather curious sight… An elderly sardarji with a pretty heavily-loaded cycle, and the cycle had an interesting sign on it - 'All India cycle yatra.'

I was doing a good speed when I passed him, and by time I had seen him and my brain had processed what I had seen, and I became curious as who this was and what his story was - I had gone quite a bit ahead.

'I should have stopped and spoken to him' I thought. 'What a pity to have missed the chance.'

Then I realised that I am alone! It was entirely my call as to what to do! I was not with the Amigos or the Ride of Uttarakhand group or anybody else - I would not be inconveniencing anyone, and I did not need anybody's permission.

I WAS RIDING ALONE! WOOHOO!

* * *

I stopped and turned around and went back to meet the ancient cyclist on the 'All India cycle tour'. He was still standing where I had seen him, and looked fairly unhappy about something.

I greeted him and he nodded back. He was an aged sikh gentleman, wearing an ochre turban and white kurta-pyjama, and was holding an ancient ladies cycle which seemed to be very heavily laden indeed. I marvelled that this old relic could have cycled up this long and steep slope on this overloaded rattletrap of a bike!

I greeted him respectfully and struck up a conversation with him and after some reserve, he told me about himself. He was all alone in the world - once he had his own shop and a wife and kid, but when the wife and child died, he sold off his shop and disposed of all his possessions and decided to travel the country on a cycle - going from pilgrimage point to pilgrimage point. He had been doing this for many years now, and had been all around the sikh pilgrimage points - Amritsar, Nanded, Patna etc etc and also to many Hindu temples and pilgrimage points as well.

'The priests know me at all the places' he said - 'at Badrinath and Kedarnath and Hemkunt sahib and Manikaran and Amritsar and everywhere. They give me a place to stay and food to eat. While travelling, I meet all kinds of people - some people just look at me and go away, while some people give me lots of love and take into their houses and insist that I eat and stay with them'

'Is that so?'

'Oh yes. Many times it has happened that the owner of the palatial kothi made me sleep in his bed, while he himself slept on the floor!'

The conversation continued for a bit and he told me about his yoga practise and life philosophy - but with a caveat.

'Will you listen?' he demanded. 'Most young people don't listen! They just want to take a photo of me, and then they zoom off!'

'Certainly I will listen.' I replied. 'I am all ears.'

He looked at me doubtfully for a bit - probably wondering if I was all tummy or all ears! But then he dropped his pearls.

'The secret of life is to meditate. But how do you meditate? People teach you all kinds of techniques - they are all bullshit. It is like trying to hold a fistful of sand! The harder you press, the faster the sand will fall out. The trick is to achieve a blank mind -

that is true meditation! Shoonyabodh! That is what you should aim for. That comes with quietness of mind.'

But the poor guy seemed to have lost his own quietness of mind. His cycle had broken down and he was not able to get it fixed - the various cycle mechanics said that this was such an old model that parts were not available! And he was bitter about the manager of the sikh dharamshala he had stayed in, where the manager had apparently ignored him and concentrated on buttering up rich pilgrims from whom he was hoping to get some money.

There was a huge truck parked behind the cycle. I was not the only guy who had noticed this old sardarji - the kind-hearted truck driver had also seen him and had stopped to help. But how to help? There was no room in the truck to load the cycle.

'Leave the bike here and go with the truck dude to the nearest town and come back with a mechanic.' I suggested.

'Leave the bike here!' he roared 'Never! It will be looted bare! All the local people are vicious thieves.'

I looked at that rotten old bike doubtfully. Only a really committed thief would touch it. But for the old dude - it was his entire life's possessions.

'Wait here and flag down a tempo and ask him to give you and bike a lift.' I suggested

'Nobody will help!' he snapped. 'All the people here are vicious and selfish.'

'Hmmm...' I thought a bit, and then said 'Come with me on my bike to the nearest town and bring back a mechanic. This truck dude will stand here and guard your bike.'

'Leave my bike? Never!' he snapped again.

Ah...the poor guy had gone into a really bad mental space.

He was filled with rage and bitterness and frustration. Poor guy. All alone in the world - no family, no friends, no home of his own…and he must be 80 years old at least. He had been wandering the roads for so long, that the thrill of doing something new and adventurous must have worn thin - and maybe he was wondering whether his choice of becoming a bairagi wanderer was the right one.

What does a man of faith do when he loses his faith? What is left?

Only time could heal him. I thought that he might feel better after a good rest and some food, and offered him some money which he accepted with a businesslike air. The trucker also gave him some money - so the old dude was sorted for the next few days at least.

I said my goodbyes and set off on my bike.

As I rode along I thought of the two mendicants I had met - the sadhus and the cyclist.

The sadhus seemed happier - but then, they were much younger and stronger than that old gentleman. I hope that all three find the divine realisation they are seeking.

By the time I reached Joshimath, it was getting dark and I hunted for a hotel. The main market area seemed to be too crowded, so I rode right to the end of town where I finally found a nice place and checked in.

The days ride was done! I was at Joshimath!

one man rides alone

Joshimath to Ghangria

I got up the next day full of excitement! I was going to explore all kinds of exciting places!

Joshimath is a staging point for various destinations - One road will take you to the ancient Badrinath temple, and to Mana village - the last village in India before the border with Tibet at Mana pass. Between Joshimath and Badrinath is the turnoff to go to the famous 'Valley of flowers' and the sikh shrine of Hemkunt sahib.

And if you take the other road, you go to Auli - the largest ski-resort of India, and further to Niti pass - another border with Tibet.

Joshimath itself is the winter abode of the Badrinath shrine - the lord symbolically moves down to Joshimath village for the winter, when the Badrinath valley is covered in snow. Joshimath - or 'Jyotirmath', as it was known in ancient times - was chosen by the great Hindu revivalist sage Adi Shankaracharya as the location of one his four main bases - or 'mathas' - to spread Hinduism…the others being at Karnataka, Dwarka in Gujarat and Puri in Odisha.

Adi Shankaracharya was a most remarkable personality - he was born in what is now Kerala, and lived only 33 years. But in that short time he became the most learned Hindu scholar in the country and defeated all other great minds in debates, travelled (on foot!) all over India, reversed the spread of Buddhism and re-established Hinduism as the pre-eminent religion in the subcontinent, and unified the various streams of Hinduism and established a whole new philosophy of 'Advait Vedanta'.

* * *

The interesting thing he did was to set up these four bases in the four corners of the subcontinent.

The first thing that struck me is that he did the whole thing on foot! By God! And then he was so influential that the kings and the hyper-conservative holy men and brahmins of the day respected him enough to allow him to establish his own bases in their domains!

Just imagine - a skinny South-Indian Malayali kid walking into the Himalayan kingdom of Garhwal more than a 1000 miles away from his hometown and demanding that he be allowed to set an independent base in a place where he did not even know the local language! He must have been a super-scholar of Sanskrit, which probably would be the 'lingua franca' of the learned people - but how did he communicate with the local people? Did he learn Gujarati, Hindi, Kumaoni, Garhwali, Odiya and all the languages in between as well as Malayalam, Kannada, Tamil, Telugu … or Prakrit or Modi or whatever the proto-languages of the time were? An intriguing thought…

In order to ensure that the local mathas remain independent and not come under the control of local pandits, he decreed that the priests at Badrinath be drawn only from the Namboodri community of Kerala! And this has remained in force till today. The priests at Badrinath are still from Kerala. (And I assume that they can speak Hindi…)

The original priests or 'Rawal's of Badrinath were Namboodiri 'Dandi sanyasis' from Kerala. When the last of the ascetics died without an heir in 1776 AD, the King of Garhwal invited non-ascetic Nambudiris from Kerala for the priesthood, a practice that continues in modern times. The selection of priest used to be done after consultation between the Garhwal and Travancore royal families. Now the process is managed by the state government rather than the royal families.

The Rawal is requested by the Government of Uttarakhand from the Government of Kerala. The candidate should possess a degree of Acharya (Post Graduate) in Sanskrit, be a bachelor, well-versed in reciting mantras (sacred texts) and be from the Vaishnava sect of Hinduism. The erstwhile ruler of Garhwal, who is the tutelary head of Badrinath, approves the candidate sent by the Government of Kerala. A Tilak Ceremony is held to instate the Rawal and he is deputed from April to November when the temple remains open. The Rawal is accorded 'his holiness' status by the Garhwal Rifles and the state government of Uttarakhand - and is allowed a staff composed of local people to help him carry out his duties.

* * *

Earlier the Rawal was the absolute boss of the temple - which meant that he was in control of the money! Now everyone wants control of the money in their own grubby little hands - so the government stepped in and took control of the place by passing the 'Shri Badarinath and Shri Kedarnath Mandir Act' and brought the money and management control of the temple under the aegis of a committee which is nominated by the State government.

Talking about Keralites in North India - I was about to get a Keralite companion of my own! Talk about Serendipity!

I had chatted with the hotel owner the earlier night to get local information about the place - how to visit, where to visit and so on - and in the morning he came to me and said
'I have good news for you!'
'Oh? Whats that?'
'I have found you a travelling companion!'
He introduced me to a tall and bearded young man, who gave me a shy smile.
'He is also crazy...er....what I mean is ...he is also a biker like you, and he is also travelling alone. And he is also headed to Badrinath. Why dont you two get together?'

The genial young man was called George, and he was a dude after my own heart! He was an Enfield rider and was out on an adventure of a lifetime! What a ride! Wow!
He had been on the road for 75 days already! He had set out from his hometown in Kerala and gone down south to Kanya Kumari, then gone up the east coast - Tamil Nadu, Andhra Pradesh, Orissa, West Bengal - the explored the North Eastern states - Assam, Meghalaya, Manipur, Nagaland etc - then went

to Bhutan. Then he had crossed the whole of India and ridden east to west to Gujarat! Then he went up to Rajasthan, Amritsar, Chandigarh, Manali and Leh - and was now with me in Joshimath, Uttarakhand!

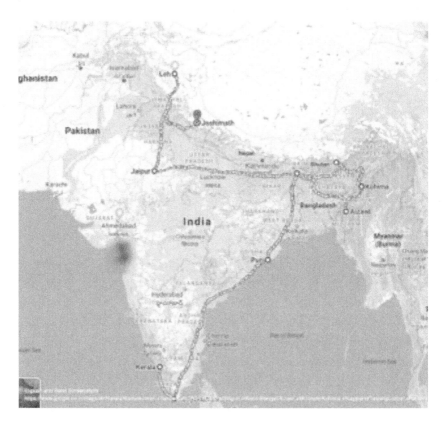

Wow! What a trip! I was in love!

(No - Not with George...with the idea of his trip!)

Poor old George - or poor young George, I should say - must have gulped a bit at the idea of travelling with a crazy fat old biker, but he rallied splendidly and declared politely that he would be charmed to travel with me.

This is one of the great joys of solo travel - you are able to mix freely with others instead of being tied up within your own group, and can join with random people on impulse.

We packed up and hit the road for Badrinath - and what an awesome road it was!

WOOHOO! WHAT A BEAUTIFUL ROAD!

That road climbed and climbed from Joshimath at 1875 meters to Badrinath at 3135 meters above MSL, and the mountainous landscape was a thing of rare beauty. I went aah and ooh at every step, and every time we crossed one of those awesome bridges, I would stop to take in the views.

* * *

Finally, I could bear it no longer and stopped on an awesome bridge, and got off the bike to revel in the view - much to George's amusement. I told him that one should ride slow and stop often to ensure that your mind is attuned to appreciating the beauty and taking in the view, rather than get stuck in a transactional view of covering distances and reaching destinations.

'The point in our trip is not the destination' I explained to him. 'It is the journey.'

That seemed to resonate with him quite a bit, and he shook my hand solemnly.

Soon after the bridge we came to Gobindghat and I was overjoyed to see a helicopter taking off!

WOOHOO!
IT'S ON! IT'S ON!

In my conversation with the hotel guy at Joshimath, I had expressed my interest in trekking to the Valley of flowers. He had looked at me doubtfully, and told me that the trek starts from a place called Gobindghat and it would take 3 days to trek to the VoF.

Three Days! My heart sank. That was too long.

But there was a helicopter option. One could take a chopper to the halfway point - from Gobindghat to Ghangria. This would save me one day going and one day coming. But he didn't know whether the service was operational or not.

AND IT WAS! WOOHOO!

* * *

'Yes!' I said, punching the air. 'Let's check it out.'

We went to the office and they said that indeed the service was on - and it operated at fixed intervals throughout the day. But they didn't take advance bookings as they could not guarantee whether the helicopter will ply or not - it was all dependent on the weather. If the weather was fine, the the bird would fly - if not - then…well…it's marching time! One Two - One Two - Left Right!

Did I want to go now?

I thought about it, and said - No - Let me go and visit Badrinath and Mana first, and then make my way down.

Me and George continued up that fantastic road - and soon we were at Badrinath! WOOHOO!

JAI BADRI VISHAL!

But I thought that we should visit Mana village first and finish seeing that, and then come down and take darshan of Lord Badrinath, and then carry on down to Gobind ghat to catch that chopper. The last flight of the chopper was by 4-ish, as it would obviously not fly in such mountainous terrain in poor visibility - and so we had a hard deadline.

I also wanted to go to Mana village first - because I wanted to check out the scene of riding to Mana pass!

Mana village is referred to - and very loudly refers to itself - as the 'Last village of India'. Everything is 'the last so and so in India' - the last restaurant, the last dhaba, the last cold drink shop, the last pan wala, the last toilet ...

But a more accurate way of putting it would be to call it 'the last major village in India on this particular border which is open to access to all Indians.' This is because there is a long road which runs from Mana village to Mana pass - which is the actual border with Tibet, and there are a couple of small hamlets and settlements on that road.

This was a standard trade route with Tibet in the old days, and merchants and travellers used to march up and down it regularly. But alas - after the Chinese invaded Tibet, all borders were slammed shut! The Chinese shut the border because it did not want Tibetans to run away into India by this pass - and the Indians closed it because they didn't want the Chinese army to be invading down it!

What a great pity! All beautiful places in the Himalayas are polluted by this border conflict with Pakistan and China. Why can't everyone bugger off and sit peacefully at home with a cold beer and some tandoori chicken? So much effort is spent in being unhappy and grasping - why can't they spend it in being happy and contented?

I was very keen to ride to Mana pass - as it would be a great adventure!

Mana pass is one of the highest vehicle-accessible passes in the world - and depending on how your GPS and altimeter are acting up - is even higher than the famous Khardung La pass! Mana pass is at 5632 meters, as compared to 5359 meters of Khardungla. This pass was the link between Uttarakhand and the ancient Tibetan kingdom of Guje - and was the route taken by the famous Portuguese travellers - the Jesuit priests António de Andrade and Manuel Marques, who were the first Europeans to enter Tibet in 1624. It was in regular use till the Chinese shut the door in 1951.

I really wanted to do this ride - but there were several complications.

The first and most obvious one was that civilians were not allowed on this road. The Indian and Chinese armies have both been breathing heavily and rattling sabres at each other lately, and so they had banned civilian traffic on this sensitive road.

The second issue was that I was alone! Practically speaking this would be an issue if I had a breakdown or an accident - or even a simple puncture - I would be stuck. And screwed. Even if the army guys did relent and give permission, they would probably allow a group but not a single guy.

The third - and most pressing - was that my bike was in a bad way! The chain was making the most alarming sounds and I frequently scared poor George who was riding behind me - who thought that my bike was about to break into two or something! I cursed the Royal Enfield team of the Ride of Uttarakhand at great length! I had told that moron mechanic repeatedly about my chain issues and that I was going on a solo ride and needed a dependable bike, and he had assured me that there would be no trouble. I had told the ride leader about it, and he had also ignored it completely. Bloody irresponsible idiots.

But hey…what you gonna do? You have to do the best with what you have got.

First I tried riding confidently into the Mana pass road! Sometimes this tactic works wonders! Just ride confidently into a gate as if you belong there - and the guard will also think you belong there and let you in with a salute!

* * *

And it is always easier to apologise than to take permission.

But alas - this trick does not work with soldiers. They follow their orders to the letter and no amount of blandishments will move them. They were polite - but extremely firm - and pointed me to Mana village.

Oh well, I had expected that - the frontal assault rarely works. I would try some other way to get permission to enter that road. Time for plan B.

And anyway, my bike was in no condition to be going up muddy mountain passes. I would have to get the bike fixed before I could try adventuring. I hoped that there was a decent bike guy at Joshimath.

We went off to explore Mana village - the last village of India. Outside vehicles are not allowed inside that village, so we parked our bikes in the last parking lot of India. Then we had a quick chai in the last chai shop of India (or possibly, the last-but-one chai shop of India) and walked along the last footpath of India....

* * *

Mana valley should actually be known as the Saraswati valley - as it the last place where one can find the fiercely flowing Saraswati river.

The Saraswati was a major river in Vedic times, and was one of the cradles of ancient civilisation. The river was as holy as - or even holier than - the Ganga and the Jamuna rivers and the Mahaprayag at Allahabad was supposed to be a 'triveni sangam' or 'confluence of three rivers' - the Ganga, Jamuna and Saraswati.

The Saraswati river was important enough to be identified as the goddess of wisdom and learning.

Then god knows what massive earth-changing event occurred to kill the river altogether - and the entire river dried up and vanished! The river has vanished so thoroughly that experts cannot even say with any certainty as to where the river used to flow - and only have a bunch of educated guesses - some say that it was the Ghaggar river which flowed between the Yamuna and the Sutlej. The Ghaggar used to flow into western India, and watered the states of Rajasthan and Kutch, Gujarat. There are a number of Harappan cities along the course of the river - at Kalibangan (Rajasthan), Banawali and Rakhigarhi (Haryana), Dholavira and Lothal (Gujarat) - all of which died out when the river dried up. The fertile plains of Rajasthan are now the Thar desert, and the green fields of Kutch are the salt marshes of the Rann of Kutch.

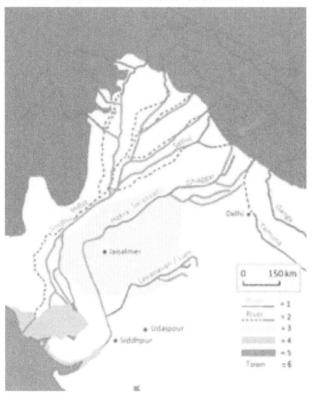

A cynic could say that the dying out of the 'goddess of wisdom' is emblematic of India today! There is no more wisdom, and all that is left is an intellectual desert...

But I am not a cynic - and will point to the powerful and strong Saraswati that I saw at Mana village! The river exists - it has just gone underground and feeding the aquifers of India now, and ensuring that there is the water of wisdom for all - you just need to dig for it!

This area is also identified with the last travels of the Pandavas of the Mahabharata epic. As I mentioned earlier, the Mahabharata war was a war fought for the succession of the kingdom of Hastinapur - between two sets of cousins, the children of two brothers Pandu and Dhritarashtra.

The children of Pandu - the Pandavas- won the war…but only by killing off all their 99 cousins and their uncles and grand-uncles and cousins-once-removed and brothers-in-law and sundry large chunks of their extended family. The Pandavas themselves lost their own sons and cousins and relatives and friends in the war - and after they had won, felt very bad about the whole thing. What was the point?

Like many winners of vicious family feuds, they wondered if they had done the right thing - and after taking over the kingdom and stabilising the place after such a brutal war, and enjoying the peace for some years - decided to leave everything and go to the mountains and try to look for some way to expiate their sins. They handed over the reins of the kingdom to a grandson, and took off their fancy clothes and their crowns and ornaments - and left their fancy palaces behind as they became ascetics and walked to the Himalayas to cleanse their souls.

They made their way here - and saw that there was no path across the fearsome chasm of the raging Saraswati - and so Bheema - the world's strongest man - lifted a giant rock and placed it over the river to make a bridge across it.

This rock (which may of course be just a natural rock arch

formation) is called the 'Bheempul' (Bheema's bridge) and is one of the sights to see here. We were lucky enough to see a beautiful little rainbow below the Bheempul! Scientifically, it was just a refraction of light through the water drops thrown up by the waterfall - but emotionally, I felt that it was a beautiful show that the Saraswati put up just for my enjoyment!

So lovely!

Bheempul is the last place where you can see the Saraswati - as it merges into the beautiful Alaknanda just outside Mana, and that confluence is a lovely sight!

There is a trail from Bheempul to a waterfall called Vasudhara falls - but it was a bit of a distance away, and my motorbiking boots were not the best option for walking so far. I could also say that we did not have much time to spare for the trek - but I suppose that me being fat and lazy also had a role to play! But we did did go for a walk for some time along that route, just to enjoy the scenery and revel in the views of the young Alaknanda flowing below. It was an amazing sight!

George had read about a shopkeeper in Mana who had a tea shop called - what else... 'The last shop in India'. George had read about him in a Malayali newspaper back in Kerala! That was because that shopkeeper's son had studied in the prestigious Indian Institute of Technology in Palakkad, Kerala. We went off in search of the shop. We had a bit of a job finding him, as now every shop is the 'last shop' - but we found him at last. George greeted him - and was delighted to see that the shopkeeper also had a copy of that Malayali newspaper! He had put up that yellowing old newspaper with great pride - and George was overjoyed to see this relic of his native land in far-off Uttarakhand. 'The last Malayali newspaper of India' perhaps?

'Where is your son now?' I asked him.

'Oh, he is in the US now.' The shopkeeper replied with quiet pride.

'Wow. That's wonderful!' I said. 'Won't you go to stay with him in America?'

'Oh no, no… I am best-off here…' he replied with a smile.

The other thing to see in Mana was the 'Vyasa gufa' the cave where Sage Vyasa is supposed to have written the Mahabharata. Well…he didn't actually write it himself… the Mahabharata is a humongous tome of 1.8 million words! 10 times the length of the Iliad and Odyssey combined! 4 times the length of the Ramayana!

'I have this awesome epic in my head' he must have said to the gods. 'But the very idea of writing it down makes my hands pain. I need a stenographer!'

Poor guy - he might have been hoping to get a hot chick as a secretary / stenographer …but to his disappointment, it was the pot-bellied elephant-headed Ganapati (remember him from earlier?) who volunteered.

'I will do it!' he trumpeted, and Vyasa must have sighed.

'Can't the divine courtesans like Rambha or Menaka do it….oh all right…but be warned! It's a long job! I am all bubbling with creativity. Get a good pen - don't get one which will get worn out!'

'No worries, dude.' Ganpati said - and broke off one of his tusks with loud CRACK and made Vyasa wince.

'Ugh! What did you do that for? Now I am feeling all queasy… I have been putting off going to the dentist for so long…'

'Can't get a more durable pen! Genuine ivory! C'mon…let's get to work!'

They gathered up a sufficient amount of writing material and got to work - 1.8 million words must have left Vyasa with a hell of a sore throat! And even Ganapati must have ended up with cramps in his hand!

The cave was… just a cave…well duh! What did I expect?…

That was it for Mana village, and we made tracks for the parking lot. As I reached close to the parking, I put my hand in my pocket…and a cold hand gripped my heart!

Where were my bike keys?

Oh shit, Oh shit, Oh shit…

The bike keys were missing!

'What?' George asked me in surprise. 'What happened?'

* * *

'I…er…seemed to have dropped my bike keys somewhere…' I said

'What?!' We stood and thought of all the places we had been to…the walk from the parking lot to Mana, Bheempul, the Vasudhara waterfall trail, that shop, Vyas gufa…it could have fallen anywhere! Where should we go and look?

Shit!

'When do you remember seeing it last?' he asked me, and I racked my brain.

'Let's see…I got off the bike and put the key in my pouch… hang on…I don't remember putting the key in the pouch…' I suddenly looked up. 'I don't remember putting the key in the pouch! Maybe I forgot the key on the bike itself!'

We sprinted (waddled?) to the bike - and I heaved a sigh of relief to see the bike still there!
I heaved another sigh of relief to see the key still in the bike!
And then I gasped - when I saw that I had left the headlight on!

Oh no! I had left the light on! I hope the battery has not been drained!

I pressed the starter - and the bike just replied with a reluctant 'gnnn'…the battery was dead!

Damn and blast!

* * *

I swore freely, and again George asked 'What?'

'The battery is drained! I left the light on!'

'Oh no…what to do now?' he asked politely.

'Er…you will have to push the bike till it starts.'

'OH NO!' he recoiled at the thought of pushing this giant fat dude and his giant bike!

He gulped a bit - but suddenly brightened up. 'Ah…the road runs downhill from here…just start your bike rolling and put it gear…it will start.'

'Ah yes…' I said in relief 'A brilliant idea!' I had also been feeling very guilty about asking a guy I had just met to push my bike around, and this felt like the perfect solution.

I did that - the bike started rolling downhill in neutral and roared happily to life as I put it in gear! WOOHOO! THE BIKE WAS BACK ON! WOOHOO!

Thank goodness for the patron saint of Idiots! I left the bike on for sometime and rode around in circles to charge the battery.

We rolled down to Badrinath and parked our bikes in front of a dhaba and went inside for lunch. My usual tactic in such a place is to park in front of such an open dhaba and then become bonafide customer by having a meal there. Then the dhaba guy will keep an eye on your bike, and many times you can stow your riding gear in the dhaba as well - helmets, jackets and stuff! That stuff will not be allowed inside the temple for security reasons, and will be safer inside a building than on the bike.

The dhaba guys were happy to see us - most people are happy to see bikers! There is something wonderfully adventurous and romantic about long distance motorcycling which really appeals to people. They asked us where we were from - and were quite incredulous when they learnt that George had come all the way from Kerala on his bike!

But after we had our lunch, the dhaba guy quietly dropped a bombshell on us.

'By the way - the temple is closed now.'

'Eh? Closed? Why?'

'The temple is always closed from 1 to 4 - it is time for the lord's siesta.'

The lord's siesta! I clutched my forehead! I had forgotten this facet of north Indian temples. The temple priest needs a nap, and says that the lord is the one taking 40 winks and locks and bolts the door!

Shit! This plays havoc with the plan! If the temple opens after 4, then there will be no time for us to take the darshan and still make it down to Govindghat in time for the helicopter.

Hmmm. I thought about it - and then decided to ditch the temple for today and go to Govindghat instead. I would anyway be coming back here for my Mana pass attempt - I would see it then.

And we might as well take advantage of the low crowd situation - as the temple was closed, all the pilgrims and visitors had dispersed. Most of the crowd was day trippers and they would have already been to the temple and left for the day. This would be a good time to check out the exteriors of the temple - and meet the Rawal of the temple... a malayali compatriot of George's.

There was a hot spring there - the 'tapt kund' - which was supposed to be part of the visit. You are supposed to take a holy dip in the sulphur waters and refresh and relax yourself before entering the temple. Hot springs are holy in India - the whole concept of unlimited hot water gushing out of the ground in these cold Himalayan heights is a miracle! But when we went to check it out, it looked cloudy and rather unhygienic - and anyway, we didn't have the time to have a relaxed dip.

We found the Keralite Rawal and greeted him and George enjoyed the novelty of speaking in his mother tongue to a fellow Keralite after 75 days on the road. The Rawal was equally happy I hope - though he restrained his enthusiasm on seeing me.

We admired the decor of the temple and then left for the chopper station at Govind ghat.

Au revoir Baba Badrinath - I shall return! In a couple of days, hopefully.

We reached Govind ghat - and man, was I relieved that we going down all the way! My chain was making really scary noises now and I could hear them even over the sound of the thumping engine. I cursed that Royal Enfield Ride of Uttarakhand team once more - but what choice was there?... keep going... I thought that even if the ruddy chain snaps in half, I could at least roll down to Joshimath in neutral.

* * *

We reached the helicopter taxi office and went in again to check it out - and I was quite taken aback to see that the company operating it was Air Deccan!

Air Deccan! Really? Wow!

The original Air Deccan company was the company that really shook up the Indian aviation scene in 2003 and opened up the skies for all with its bold low-cost approach. The company was founded by a most remarkable person - Captain G R Gopinath, formerly of the Indian Army.

Captain Gopinath was an alumnus of the National Defence Academy and the Indian Military Academy and fought in the 1971 Indo-Pak war, which resulted in the formation of Bangladesh. But after 8 years, he left the Army and decided to strike out on his own.

He tried various businesses - he started one of first ecologically sustainable sericulture farms in India (for which he was awarded the Rolex Laureate award in 1996), then opened a hotel - and most interestingly - became a Royal Enfield dealer! That company - Malnad Mobikes - is still a big Enfield dealer in Hassan, Karnataka!

After dealing with Royal Enfield, he must have thought that he can do anything!

In 1992, He bumped into a friend of his from the Army - Captain K J Samuel - who was a helicopter pilot, and was planning to start his own commercial helicopter service. They must have discussed and thought about this for years - because when the Indian government rolled out aviation reforms in 1995 to promote private entrepreneurship, they got together to start a helicopter service called Deccan Aviation. This business did very well - they got a lot of business from fly-happy politicians and businessmen, and also a lot of rescue and support work in Sri Lanka, Nepal, Kabul and South India. The Company grew to become one of the largest private air charter company in India and Sri Lanka.

Inspired by this success - and inspired by the stories of successful low-cost operators like Southwest Airlines and such - he decided to start his own low-cost airline! He called it Air Deccan, and said that he is going to open up the skies for the poor people. The fares will be low enough to enable the lower segments of the population to fly - and this will be such a huge population that even the wafer-thin margins would be enough to have a profitable business.

And wow - did he shake up the market! Air Deccan tore up the market with its spectacularly low fares - and Me and Bharathi were its enthusiastic customers! He launched a loss-leader scheme of offering one ticket at Re 1 only... chosen by random draw…and once I was lucky enough to get one of those! I flew Bombay Hyderabad for just Rs 221! Rs 220 for the taxes and Re 1 for the fare! That was cheaper than a second-class train ticket! (Now of course, the taxes themselves are in the thousands…)

Within 3 years he had become the 3rd largest airline in India, with a 19% market share. The airline bet big on expansion and ordered billions of dollars worth of aeroplanes and hired staff and bought offices and all that stuff. He opened up lots of under-served routes and tried a lot of unconventional ideas to cut costs and operate at low margins - he was a true pioneer of Indian aviation!

But this runaway success attracted a lot of competition - and a lot of unwelcome attention as well! The airline was hounded by the government - whether due to suggestion from competitors or for bribes - and found itself in a tight spot. The government behaved like a real scumbag and forced the airline into the red.

He was targeted for a takeover by the liquor baron Vijay Mallya, who had launched the finest full-service airline of the time - Kingfisher airways. Gopinath tried to reason with Mallya that he was a no-frills economy airline, while Kingfisher was a luxurious full-service line and their DNA was totally different… but Mallya wouldn't listen and kept leaning on him.

As Captain Gopinath was not politically connected, and not a hoodlum - he couldn't stand up to all the pressures, and agreed to sell off the airline to Kingfisher.

Unfortunately for the Indian flyer - all that happened is that

India lost its best low-cost airline as well as its best full-service airline. Kingfisher couldn't absorb the acquisition - and Mallya himself was hounded by the government and the banks (I told you the government is a scumbag) and the airline went bust and Mallya went bankrupt and had to sell off all his assets and flee the country.

An extremely sad story - Indian aviation's biggest problem is the Indian government.

Gopinath managed to save the helicopter charter business from the Kingfisher fiasco and is now running services with helicopters and small fixed-wing planes at various places in India - doing these little short-hop flights - and probably dreaming of restarting his airline some day.

Poor Captain Gopinath!

I went inside and asked about the fares.

'Well sir...' he looked at me and smirked. 'The fare is only Rs 2875...'
'Hey...that's not bad!' I said, smiling. 'That's very reasonable.'
'...upto 80 kgs.'
'Eh?'
'I mean that the fare is a flat rate of Rs 2875 if the passenger weighs less than 80 kgs.'
'Eh? And if he weighs more than 80 kgs?'
'Then we charge per kilogram extra.'
'WHAT!'
'Yes you fat slob! HAHAHAHAHA! Pay up, you lump of lard' (he didn't say that out loud - but I could hear the unsaid

words!)

I would have to pay an ass-tronomical amount because of my huge ass! Oh no!

Screw you, Captain Gopinath!

I clutched my ample adipose and reeled! I knew that being overweight will cost me in the long run - but I had no idea that it would cost me in the short run as well!

Luckily George was well below the 80 kg mark and they adjusted that against our combined total weight...but I still had to pay more than double the fare! Oh no!

The total weight was including our luggage of course, but they kindly agreed to keep our luggage and helmets and riding gear in storage with them - and I took as few clothes as possible and the copter guys had to warn me to take warm clothes as it would be cold and possibly wet up there.

The helicopter ride itself was wonderfully scenic and thrilling as we went up the valley and soon we were at Ghangria ! WOOHOO! And we had saved ourselves a day and a half of walking!

I huffed and puffed a bit as we ascended from the helipad to Ghangria village and found a nice little place to stay in.

The next day we would trek to the Valley of flowers!

Valley of Flowers

Ghangria seemed to be a town with no reason for existence except to act as a base for trekkers going to Valley of Flowers and pilgrims going to the Hemkunt gurudwara. Both of these places must have really opened up the economy of this part of Uttarakhand.

The Hemkunt pilgrimage phenomenon is something that seems to be quite recent - after the 60s. There is a beautiful lake in the Bhyundar valley - the Hem Kund or the 'Golden lake' and being a isolated lake situated in the accessible mountains, it was apparently a popular spot for the more unsociable and solitude-seeking ascetics who wanted a quiet place to meditate in.

For some strange reason, it became associated with sikhism. No guru ever went near the place - not one of them.

Even Guru Nanak - the founder of the Sikh religion - never came here. It must have been one of the few places that he had not been to, as he was a very peripatetic person, who travelled all over the known world.

So why choose the only place that he had never been to - as a pilgrimage place? So strange.

But some places just click! Most Sikh holy sites are places visited by Gurus, or birthplace or death place or battle ground or consecrated place, etc. In spite of having no direct link at all to any Sikh Guru - Hemkunt became strangely famous and developed as a pilgrimage point - for Sikhs.

It really took off when a hotshot of the Indian Army visited there in 1962 - Major General Harkirat Singh, KCIO, Engineer-in-Chief, Indian Army. The original gurudwara at the lake must have been a simple and serene place, but Harkirat decided to earn some merit - by spending the Indian Army's money - and decided to build a new and swanky gurudwara there. And so he ordered Architect Manmohan Singh Siali of the Military Engineering Services (MES) to go forth and conquer! Siali got to work and studied the place and got a firm of sikhs to build a fancy gurudwara there. This has become a pilgrimage point for the lakhs of Sikhs - and non-sikhs - who trek up there in search of merit.

But it was incredibly high up - and it would take a day of its own to climb and down (not to mention another day to work off the muscle cramps) - so I decided to give it a miss. And anyway, crowded pilgrimage trek paths are incredibly horrible and best left only to the pilgrims who dont mind profane things like litter and mule poop and noisy pilgrims and so on.

We would go and explore the lovely Valley of Flowers!

* * *

The Valley of Flowers is also a fairly recent discovery - it was discovered quite by chance by a bunch of lost mountaineers in 1931! The British mountaineers Frank S. Smythe, Eric Shipton and R.L. Holdsworth were returning from an expedition to climb Mt Kamet. Kamet is the second highest mountain in the Garhwal, after Satopanth- and in those days, before you could climb a mountain you had to find it first!

The local people had no interest in climbing these huge and inaccessible mountains - why should they? There was neither food or grazing land or farm land there. Why go? - And so there were no paths to these places. The intrepid climbers of those days used to first find a way to the mountain and then climb it - and obviously, they got lost quite often.

* * *

They stumbled on this valley while coming back - and they were lucky with the season, and the place was full of wild flowers! They were totally charmed and gave it the quite irresistible name 'Valley of Flowers'.

Dandelion

I think it's an insult
To Nature's generosity
That many call this cheerful flower
A 'common weed'.
How dare they so degrade
A flower divinely made!
Sublimely does it bloom and seed
In sunshine or in shade,
Thriving in wind and rain,
On stony soil
On walls or steps
On strips of waste;
Tough and resilient,
Giving delight
When other flowers are out of sight.
And when its puff-ball comes to fruit
You make a wish and blow it clean away:
'Please make my wish come true,' you say.
And if you're kind and pure of heart,
Who knows? This magic flower might just respond
And help you on your way.
Good dandelion,
Be mine today.

- Ruskin Bond

This name- 'Valley of flowers' - really fired the imagination of the British, who are notoriously flower-friendly - and they sent a

115

lady Botanist from the famous Kew gardens of London to study the valley in 1939. Her name was Joan Margaret Legge, and unfortunately she was not 'sure-legged' (dreadful pun ... I know) and slipped and fell - and died. Her sister (the other Legge! ... Ok Ok...I will stop) came and built a grave for her - and that has become a tourist attraction!

Soon after this incident, the (British) Government of India declared the whole Nanda Devi basin as a 'Game sanctuary' in 1939 and banned hunting and grazing and agriculture here to preserve the natural beauty. India became independent in 1947 - but unfortunately China attacked Tibet almost immediately and conquered it. The Dalai Lama was forced to flee, and India received him and gave him sanctuary - which cheesed off the Chinese and they ended up attacking India in 1961.

Since this area was just at the border with Tibet, the Indian army sealed off the area to Indian civilian traffic in 1962 - and kept it sealed for 10 years! They opened up to mountaineering in 1972 - and upgraded the place to a national park in 1980. It was first called the 'Sanjay Gandhi national park' - a most ugly name ! But luckily the Congress was defeated and the new ruling party changed the name of the place to the much more appealing 'Valley of Flowers national park'. This has now become one of the most popular and well-known trekking destinations in India.

And just think! If Smythe and Shipton had happened to come here just a month here and there, they would have missed all the flowering - the place is worth seeing only in August end - and would have thought of it as just another valley and it would be completely unknown today!

We got up early in the morning and set out at first light! We fortified ourselves with a piping-hot aloo-paratha breakfast, full of grease and carbs to fuel us for a long day. We shared the trail with the pilgrim gang for a short distance and even at that early hour it was full of pilgrims. Some were bouncing up, some were trudging up grimly, some were on the mules and ponies who had shat liberally all over the path (the ponies shat - not the pilgrims) (I sure hope so) - and some were being carried up by porters! One could either sit in a palanquin with four porters carrying you - an expensive affair! They charged Rs 20,000 for weight upto 80 kilos, with extra charge for more weight! A cheaper option was that one porter strapped a bamboo chair on his back and you sat in that chair and the porter carried you up on his back! It all looked extremely uncomfortable - and expensive - and I wondered whether one really acquires merit when one goes to a pilgrimage point carried on someone else's back?

I mean - you go to all that expense and discomfort - and when you die you find that the porter is the one who acquired the merit? What a disappointment that would be!

I was most happy when the paths diverged and the traffic dropped sharply once we were off the pilgrim trail. There were no ponies - and therefore no pony dung on the trail - and that was a great improvement. The silence was amazing - and walking in the mountains is always awesome. We were following the swift-flowing Pushpawati river now, which drains the valley of flowers. The Pushpawati rises from the east Kamet glacier on the Indo-Tibet border and flows through the valley of flowers to join the Bhyundar river near Ghangria - the combined stream is called the Laxman Ganga, and that joins the Alaknanda at Govind ghat.

The word 'Pushpawati' means 'Flower river' - and that must have inspired Smythe to name the valley as he did. Interestingly, the Pushpawati was first explored in modern times in 1862 by another guy with a very similar name - Smyth - Col. Edward Smyth. So Smyth and Smythe are the godfathers of the Valley of Flowers!

Sadly, we were at the wrong time to visit the VoF - the peak of the flowering happens in August - and we were in September. 'There are no flowers now' was something said to us many times in Ghangria - most strangely by a guy who offered to be our guide.

I was actually willing to take a guide - I normally like to take local guides…it helps the local economy and you can get to see and appreciate things which you might miss as a casual walker.

But this guy de-sold himself spectacularly by telling us repeatedly that there are no flowers now - but I will take you if you wish. Are you sure you want a guide? Are you really sure? Come back and tell me if you are sure! Oh you dont want to take a guide? Good good… there are no flowers now…

What a strange fellow…

We crossed that powerful river over a rather rickety-looking bridge and continued along the trail. That flowing river was amazingly beautiful and I really had to tear myself away from there! But I thought that it might be better to press on now - we could always chill out here on the way back.

The only problem was the track. Instead of leaving it as a normal soil path, they had dumped an awful lot of rock over it to make it a disgusting rocky path - which was awful to walk on! The rocks were sharp and pointy and slippery - they poked you through and through the thin soles of my sneakers, and you had to carefully weave your way through them to avoid a nasty slip and fall on the wet and slippery stones.

They should have either left it as it is, or made the effort of making a nice path with cobblestones or gravel - or wooden planks. What is the point of dumping a lot of unfinished stone and leaving it? Stupid bloody assholes. Somebody must have complained of the path being a muddy mess, and the local government officer must have been commanded to build a path - and he had done as shoddy a job of it as he could. Or perhaps the contractor had pocketed the cost of finishing the path, and the government official must have signed off on it as stamped it as being finished.

The path seemed to be going straight up! It climbed and climbed steadily - and that pointy rocky road made it more difficult that a normal path would have been. I could see that

George was holding back because of me - and I told him to go on ahead at his natural pace - I would catch up, never fear.

He gave my portly frame a doubtful look - will this lump of lard make it?

Hah! I will show you! Fat people can trek too!

I climbed on grimly - like Samwise Gamgee climbing the Misty mountains after Frodo - and concentrated on putting one foot after another.

That's all that it takes to climb the steepest hill. Just keep putting one step after another.

Count to 500 steps, and then take a breather - and then walk another 500 steps. And repeat.

* * *

Slow and steady may not not win the race - but you don't need to win it…only to complete it!

In fact, this can help you to enjoy the walk more…when you are walking slow you can take the time to look around and enjoy the sights of the road. See the scenery - the far-off mountains, the blue sky, the shy green leaf just budding on the tree, a frog looking at you enquiringly, an interesting stone… even the smallest things can be the most beautiful.

The trail climbed straight up for 3 kilometres! Steep and rocky steps added to the challenge, not to mention the rain and the water flowing down the steps. I wondered about coming here in August - that would be the peak of the monsoon, and this trail would be even more difficult at that time…with waterfalls of water flowing down these rocky steps. And wouldn't it be a shame if you came all this way and the whole valley was covered in rainclouds and you didn't see a thing?

But then - showing beautiful views is god's work…your job is to complete the journey.

Finally I completed that climb and entered the valley! WOOHOO! I HAD DONE IT! I HAD DONE IT! WOO HOO!

Now I was in the Valley of Flowers - and what a lovely sight it was!
Beautiful! Fantastic!

The sky was blue and clear, with cotton wool clouds accenting it - and the valley was green and verdant with grass. You could see the lovely Pushpawati river running through it below and the great mountains of the Garhwal Himalayas made a majestic backdrop. It was simply awe-inspiring!

There were not many people on the trail - and it was quiet and serene. The government had put up painted signs to urge the trekkers to chill out and relax and soak in the scenery.

'Stay a while and enjoy the view of the Tipra glacier' one sign said. 'This is the blue poppy area'

Alas- this was where a guide would have been useful - I didn't know the names of flowers…as far I was concerned it was blue flower, pink flower, red flower, yellow flower etc. A knowledgeable guide would have told the names of the flowers, and perhaps some little tidbit about them.

This valley was part of the Nanda Devi biosphere and was representative of the 'Western Himalayan alpine shrub and meadows ecoregion' and has a number of habitats including 'valley bottom, river bed, small forests, meadows, eroded, scrubby and stable slopes, moraine, plateau, bogs, stone desert and caves'. It has scads and scads of varieties of flowers and shrubs and ferns and thingumajigs out there - a boffin called C P Kala studied the place for 10 years and counted over 520 species of higher plants - many of which are found only here.

Imagine that - people study this place for 10 years and know 520 species - and all I knew was red flower, pink flower, yellow flower...

Oh well...to each his own.

The valley extends for 5 kilometres - which would have been far more enjoyable without those god-awful rocks on the path - and I enjoyed myself strolling along that path all alone, humming to myself and occasionally breaking into song and probably frightening wildlife and trekkers alike with my discordant notes.

I stopped at the next government sign 'Stop a while and enjoy the sight of the Ratavan mountain range and Tipra glacier.' - Probably aimed at the guys who are walking grimly along determined only to reach the end of the trail as fast as possible. 'Chill out! Relax...' it seems to say - but then warns 'DONT LITTER!'
Another sign implored me to 'Sit a while and enjoy the sight of the river and streams'

I plodded happily along the path soaking in the view and taking photos. There were indeed very few flowers - just as the guide had warned us - but it was awesomely beautiful all the same. I could go on and on about the beauties of the valley - but it all gets a bit repetitive ... blue skies, puffy clouds, green grass and shrubs, winding silvery river... yadayadayada.

As George had gone on ahead, I was doing this trail all alone. While being alone has a few disadvantages - you cannot point out a beautiful thing to someone, or share some thought or - more practically - bum a drink from his water bottle!

But the advantage is that you are all alone and are silent and can just listen and take in the place with all your senses. You dont get distracted with conversation and your thoughts bounce around inside your brain.

I wandered lonely as a cloud
That floats on high o'er vales and hills,
When all at once I saw a crowd,
A host, of golden daffodils;
Beside the lake, beneath the trees,
Fluttering and dancing in the breeze.

Continuous as the stars that shine
And twinkle on the milky way,
They stretched in never-ending line
Along the margin of a bay:
Ten thousand saw I at a glance,
Tossing their heads in sprightly dance.

The waves beside them danced; but they
Out-did the sparkling waves in glee:
A poet could not but be gay,
In such a jocund company:
I gazed—and gazed—but little thought
What wealth the show to me had brought:

For oft, when on my couch I lie

In vacant or in pensive mood,
They flash upon that inward eye
Which is the bliss of solitude;
And then my heart with pleasure fills,
And dances with the daffodils.

- Wordsworth

I finally caught up with George at the end of the trail. The trail
ends at a bend in the river and you can see the Pushpavati
twisting sinuously in front of you. The road goes ever on of
course - and if you have the fitness and enthusiasm - and the
trekking permit - You can continue beyond the river and press
on to Kamet or Ratavan or Tipra glacier or wherever. But for us,
it was the end of the trail. We sat around for a bit and drank the
river water and washed our faces in that refreshing cold
mountain water.

I could hardly believe it - I had reached the end of the Valley of Flowers trek!

I had not planned for it at all - it had just happened by chance. Staying atJoshimath, chat with friendly Hotelier, meeting George, getting the Helicopter, finding Badrinath to be closed…and I had just run with it. What fun it is to just go with the flow! Life can hand you the most amazing gems just like that.

The trick is to just go for it - and figure it out as you go along.

George had made a new friend - a filmmaker called Alok - and they chatted with each other as I sat around.

Soon it was time to return, and we turned back and started our downward route. We walked back to the start of the valley and I took a last look at the majestic vista of the Ratavan range and the Tipra glacier before we started on the 3 km downward climb.

That climb down was epic - and I wondered how I had climbed up so far! One would think that climbing down would be easier than climbing up - and I suppose it is…but it is still quite demanding of the quads and calves! Quite a workout! I was quite fagged out by the time we got back to Ghangria!

I had thought of catching the last helicopter back to Govindghat, but it was too late…and anyway I was too tired as well. It would be best to chill and relax for the night here itself. I got back to the room and ordered hot water for a bath to relax my tired muscles and lay down to relax for a bit.

I was very tired and racked with cramps - but I was happy.

* * *

I had done the trek of Valley of Flowers!

WOOHOO!

The day is done, and the darkness
    Falls from the wings of Night,
As a feather is wafted downward
    From an eagle in his flight....

- Ruskin Bond

Ghangria - Joshimath - Auli

I awoke like a giant refreshed! I was cramp-free and all ready for a new day of adventure! The trek interlude was done and it was time to get back on the bike.

I had a nice hot bath and had a hot breakfast and we made our way down to the helipad for our trip back to Govindghat.

As we waited for the copter we chatted about George's awesome 75 day trip across India.

'Tell me about your adventures man - what were the good and bad experiences?'

He looked at me very seriously and said 'You know… I have not had a single bad experience! It may sound difficult to believe, but I have not had a single negative thing happen to me! People have been lovely all over India.'

'I believe it man.' I said 'I too have had only good experiences.' India is an awesome place, full of good people.

That sounds very Panglossian, I know - I am sure that what with what one reads in newspapers and sees on TV, one would think that a solo traveller is taking his life into his hands when you leave your home…but that is simply not true. As a traveller, the chances are extremely high that you will be treated with nothing but love and respect all over India. And a solo motorcyclist - even more so.

So if you are thinking of travelling India - just go for it.

I invited him to share the story of his trip on video - he was a bit shy at first, but then told his story with elan. He told me how he started from Kerala and went to Kanya Kumari, stayed at an ashram, visited the border town of Dhanushkodi, rode through TN and Andhra Pradesh to Orissa, where he visited Puri and Konark, then went to West Bengal and took a trip in a boat in the Sundarbans national park. Then he went up to Siliguri where a cousin of his joined him and they did a ride of the Northeast. They went to Cooch Behar, and then crossed the mighty Brahmaputra river in a rickety little boat at a place called Dhubri, and entered Meghalaya. Then they rode through little forested border roads which zigged and zagged through the India Bangladesh borders, explored the Siju limestone caves, Dawki river and then went on to Mizoram and admired its capital city of Aizawl. From there they entered Meghalaya and went to Loktak lake, and then to Imphal. Then they were told that the whole state was going to close down for a couple of days due to a strike, so they rode all night to get out of Meghalaya and entered Nagaland. He was just telling me about how they entered Arunachal and stayed in a fortified village - when the chopper came in and we had to cut the interview.

Unfortunately we never did get around to completing that interview - I was keen to hear the rest of the story - his ride across the country from North east India to North west India and then to up north...

We went to board our helicopter - we had already completed the ticketing when we came.

'Sir, please stand on this weighing scale so I can take your weight.' The harassed looking ticketing agent had said - and I could see George politely and heroically repressing his grin. But I just gave the guy my inward booking details and booked return tickets at the same price - so that weighing scale escaped the fate of being stepped on by the heaviest guy in the valley - it audibly creaked in relief!

* * *

The flight back was just as thrilling as the flight in - even more so, as it was in full sunlight, and we could see the beautiful LaxmanGanga valley in all its glory! What a view! What an experience!

And what a time and effort saver! That helicopter ride was what made it possible for me to the Valley of Flowers trek!

Thank you Captain Gopinath!

We landed back at Govind ghat and reclaimed our gear and our bikes, and rode back down to Joshimath.

The very first thing I needed to do was to get the bike fixed - the chain was making a very scary noise indeed! Luckily there was a bike mechanic in Joshimath, and he diagnosed my problem as a broken bearing and replaced it.

'Actually your entire chain and sprocket kit needs to be replaced...' he told me. '...but I don't have the parts. If you find a Royal Enfield service centre, then do get that done. Your chain will keep slipping as the sprocket teeth have gone.'

* * *

How could I tell that guy that I had been travelling with a
Royal Enfield service centre of the Ride of Uttarakhand for 10
days - and they still hadn't diagnosed and fixed my problem?

Now that the bike was fixed - time to handle the next task…
to get a permit to go to Mana pass!

I had asked my brother to help out - he spoke to the local
army guy, and told me that I should go to the local Sub
divisional District Magistrate at Joshimath to get a permit. I had
sent the SDM my application and details by email - but as you
can imagine, the government people weren't big users of email. I
would have to go there personally and talk to him.

George would not be coming with me - he was rushing back
home. His friends were having a get-together in three days time
and he was determined to ride out and hang with them for the
party.

'Oh? And where are you meeting them?'

'Gokarna.'

'Gokarna…GOKARNA! KARNATAKA?' I was stunned.

'Yes!' he replied happily. 'It will be great to hang out with
friends again! This trip has gone on long enough - 75 days solo.'

'You are going to ride all the way from Joshimath to
Gokarna?'

'Yes.'

'In how much time?'

'The party is in three days.'

'Wow! You are going to ride 2500 km in 3 days? Awesome.'

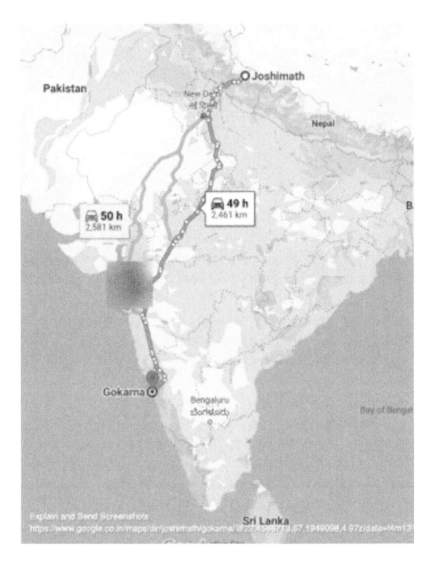

Personally, I would have just sent the bike by train and taken the flight to Goa…but George was made of sterner stuff!

We shook hands and hugged, and he zoomed off, eager to get home again after a long and epic ride. I was happy to have met him - the joys of solo travel!

* * *

And now I was alone again!

I checked in again at the same hotel, changed and went to the Sub District Magistrate office in Joshimath in search of my permit.

Unfortunately, the SDM was out of office. When will he be back? After lunch.

Hmm. No point in hanging around here then - Let me go to Auli and check it out.

As I mentioned earlier - the road splits into a Y at Joshimath. One road goes up to Badrinath and Mana, and the other road goes up to Auli and the Niti pass, which is another border pass with Tibet. Niti pass is a long way off, but Auli was just up the road, so to speak - and I would go and check that out and be back after lunch to meet the DM.

It was a very pleasant and short ride to Auli - all the more fun because I was not wearing the protective gear! Protective gear is very important and must be worn at all times during a long ride - but one cannot deny that it is more fun to ride without it … the wind plays around your body and you feel at one with the surroundings.

The road went steeply uphill and wound through a number of army / para-military establishments - and also a Skiing and Mountaineering institute of the Indo-Tibetan Border Police. The ITBP is an interesting body - it was created (raised) just after the Indo-China war in 1961 because there were a number of complicated border issues with Tibet - and the government did not want to involve the army in all of them. If your army crosses a border, then it is grounds for war. But if a police force does the same, then it is a much less serious matter and can be resolved amicably in the future. That's why you have forces like the Border Security Force (BSF). ITBP, Rashtriya Rifles etc… they are armed and dangerous - but technically, not the actual Army.

Indo-Tibetan Border Police was raised on October 24, 1962 for reorganizing the frontier intelligence and security set up along the Indo-Tibetan border. At first it was a small operation with only 4 battalions, but their role expanded over the years and now the Indian government has moved to a 'One border, one force' model and so the ITBP has been tasked with border security duty for the entire Indo-China border - 3488 kilometers!

They specialise in all kinds of high-altitude hi-jinks (I am thinking of that James Bond chase scene on skis) - and do a lot of natural disaster relief in the mountains. They did a lot of sterling work in that 2013 Uttarakhand disaster I mentioned earlier.

Auli is also the premier skiing destination in India - the only place with a chair lift apart from Gulmarg in Kashmir. It is actually a real pity that a country with as many Himalayan snow peaks as India should be so pathetically poor in skiing infrastructure - but since most of India's snowy mountains are on the border - active bubbling borders with unfriendly neighbours like China and Pakistan - the authorities clamp down heavily on high-altitude tourism… a classic case of throwing the baby out with the bathwater.

Auli does offer ski courses for beginners - but that is obviously in the winter…when there is snow! In the summer there is not much to do apart from stare at the beautiful scenery. I had lovely views of Nandadevi - the highest peak in Uttarakhand - and in fact, the highest mountain situated entirely in India. The highest peak in India is Kangchenjunga - but we share that with Nepal. I had a nice cup of tea at a friendly tea-stall and took in the views of Nandadevi before returning back to Joshimath to meet the Sub-Divisional Magistrate - the senior bureaucrat of the ...er...sub-division.

I finally managed to meet the SDM and placed my case before him of wanting a permit to ride to Mana pass on my motorcycle. There was nothing unique about this request - except for the fact that I was a lone rider. Numerous groups have done the ride to Mana pass earlier.

'You should have written to us much earlier.' He told me, irritably. 'How can you come at the last minute like this?'

I had written to him much earlier, I reminded him - but he just tchahed at me. 'Eh email... must have gotten buried somewhere...'

'You have to file a fresh application now.' He told me grandly - and so I embarked on the great activities of Indian bureaucracy...writing letters! I was first directed to a professional letter writer - who converted my simple ask of wanting a permit to go and see Mana pass into suitable officialese and relieved me of a nice tip. Then I took that letter to another dude - who wrote yet another letter. Then I attached a copy of my identification documents (I idly wondered how many forests must have fallen prey to this bureaucratic paper-eating machine till now... I personally must have submitted many hundreds of copies of my identification documents to various government departments, banks, insurance companies, financial service companies, telecom companies, airlines etc over the years. God only knows what they do with so many copies of the stuff. Why not just write down the ID number and let it go at that?)

I proudly took my collection of dead-trees to the SDM - and

he told me to get a go-ahead from the LIU!

What on earth is the LIU? I asked in puzzlement

The LIU - he told me grandly - is the 'Local Intelligence Unit'

What on earth do I have to do with a Local Intelligence Unit, when I am not a local? - How is he going to vet me when he knows nothing about me?

Tchah - he said - just get a sign-off from them and I will issue you the letter.

I sighed, and went off to find the LIU. I found the office - but it was empty! And unlocked! Nice kind of intelligence unit - I thought to myself...anybody can enter and riffle through his files. I got the guy's mobile number from a sign on the door and called him and told him that I need his sign-off for the Mana pass permit. He was out of office, he told me - he will be back by evening. He told me to leave the application on his desk and he will sign it and send it to the DM office.

What to do now? I shrugged my shoulders and went back to my hotel for a nap.

I called him again at 5 - and now he tells me that since it is pretty late, he will not be coming back to the office today, and I should come back tomorrow at noon!

What shit! That would mean that the whole of tomorrow will be wasted! Oh no!

I called up the SDM - and he got angry at me!

'Why did you waste the whole day eh? Why didn't you come and tell me that the LIU fellow is not available?'

'But...but...'

'Where is the application now?'

'Er…it's in the LIU office…'

'Go and collect it and come here right now!'

'I…er…OK…'

I rushed back, invaded the LIU office again - it was still unlocked, thank goodness! If some officious fellow had locked it and gone I would have been in the soup! I took those idiotic documents and went to the SDM's office.

The SDM gave me a dirty look.

'Finally! There you are! I waited especially for you!'

You did? I looked at the time - it was 5.30 pm.

'Which government office will you find open after 5.45 eh? I made my secretary also wait for you!'

Well - that is very true! I humbly thanked him.

'Give me the application' he said, and signed it and handed it over to his flunky - who typed out a most impressive official letter in hindi.

It said that as per your application we are granting you permission to visit Mana pass area in accordance with the Criminal Law Amendment Act 1961!

Really! The Criminal Law Amendment Act! Just to visit Mana pass! Wow!

I had permission only for one day and for me alone and I had to faithfully abide by a whole list of conditions as stated below - no photography / no sketching, drawing, painting etc. Take a fitness test, we would have to pay for any air rescue if required, the government takes no responsibility, tell the authorities before I leave…etc etc. And 11 people were copied on that document - the local police, local government officer, ITBP chappies, Army, para military forces…everyone except the local postman, it seemed to me. 11 people!

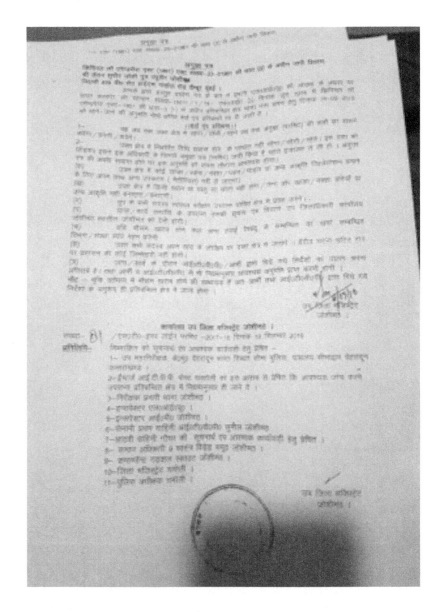

I gratefully took that document and thanked the SDM for his kind help and consideration. He had been quite a sweet guy.

Now that the work was done, the dude unbent a bit.

'Not at all, not at all…we are always happy to help tourists…see the work we did at Valley of flowers..'

I gave him a look. 'Valley of Flowers, eh?'

'Oh yes…the path was so muddy! I ordered them to pay out a stone path there - now people can walk in peace and comfort…hehe…'

So this was the guy! Gah!

I was tempted to say something, but he had genuinely helped in getting this permit.

I suppose that his heart was in the right place - so I just smiled and left, clutching my permit happily. It had taken the full day - and a lot of paper, but I had finally got the permit.

I started skipping happily beside my bike, and must have startled the onlookers quite a bit!

I WAS GOING TO MANA PASS! I WAS GOING TO MANA PASS!

WOOHOO!

Badrinath and Mana Pass

I sprang out of bed the next day, full of enthusiasm! I was going to tackle Mana pass - all alone and unsupported!

I packed up and set out for Badrinath - it was a pleasure to do that awesome ride once more. What incredible views! What a vista!

While zooming up this lovely road, one should stop and think about how difficult it was for the pilgrims in earlier days, and how simple it is now. It used to be so dangerous!

As Frank Smythe wrote... 'So they venture on their pilgrimage ... Some borne magnificently by coolies, some toiling along in rags, some almost crawling, preyed on by disease and distorted by dreadful deformities ... Europeans who have read and travelled cannot conceive what goes on in the minds of these simple folk, many of them from the agricultural parts of India, wonderment and fear must be the prime ingredients. So the pilgrimage becomes an adventure. Unknown dangers threaten the broad well-made path, at any moment the gods, who hold the rocks in leash, may unloose their wrath upon the hapless passers-by. To the European it is a walk to Badrinath, to the Hindu pilgrim it is far, far more.'

In those days people used to conduct their last rites at home before setting out for pilgrimage to these remote and forbidding Himalayan temples - as they were fully prepared not to return home. Not that they didn't want to - but the dangers were many ... natural ones like landslides and snowfall and floods and what not, diseases like Cholera, Dysentery, TB etc - and human ones like getting killed by dacoits and robbers, or strangled by thugs or whatever.

Today's pilgrims not only expect to return home - in some cases they plan to return home the very same day! A time-poor and cash-rich guy can get on a plane and reach Dehradun, and then take a helicopter to Badrinath - take the darshan and return the same day! Captain Gopinath will enable it!

Did I mention that Badrinath is a Vishnu shrine ? It is quite remarkable in a mountain area where most of the temples are Shiva temples - as befitting a God who lives alone on top of the highest mountains.

I found it quite funny that a guy known as 'Shankaracharya' (literally 'Priest of Shankara - Shiva) was actually a Vishnu devotee. Talk about misleading nomenclature.
Three of the four 'dhaam's of Shankaracharya are Vishnu temples - Badrinath (Vishnu), Dwarka (Krishna), Puri (Jagannath) - while the fourth one at Rameshwaram is technically a Shiva temple (Ramnathswamy) - but it is the place where Rama - an incarnation of Vishnu - worshipped Shiva - and hence is also a Vishnu temple.

(Just to add to the confusion - there are now two Shankaracharyas who claim to be successors of the Adi Shankaracharya - one is based at Shringeri … where the deity is neither Shiva nor Vishnu, but a goddess named Sharda - considered to be a form of Saraswati. The other Shankaracharya sits at Kanchipuram … where also the deity is a goddess, Kamakshi - a form of Durga.)

The Badrinath temple itself has no clear history - some say that it was a Buddhist temple which was converted to a Hindu temple by the Adi S. Another legend goes that the Adi S discovered some old idols in a river and placed them under a large Badri tree (Jujube or Indian date) and hence it came to be known as Badrinath. The ancient legend is that Vishnu was meditating and his consort, the Goddess Lakshmi took the form of a giant Badri tree to shield him from the sun and rain.

There apparently used to be a whole forest of these Badri trees here - but strangely, the faithful seemed to have cut down all these trees and so there is now no actual Badri around, and Badrinath - the lord of trees - is hidden inside a temple of stone. There is not a single tree left in that entire Badri complex - it's entirely a forest of buildings now - something which I thought was very sad indeed.

I reached Badrinath within hours - and again I bypassed the temple and told the lord 'first things first, O Lord…Let me do Mana pass first and then I will drop in on the way back.'

I could almost hear Badrinath snicker at me.

'First things first, eh?' I could clearly hear the words in my head. 'We shall see about that, won't we?'

Eh? What? Why? … But no reply came except for a vast feeling of amusement.

I shook my head and slapped myself on the head… I was hearing things!

But never mind - it was time to see Mana! WOOHOO! I turned confidently towards the road and immediately a soldier barred my way with an imperious hand.

* * *

'Sorry sir - you are not allowed here. Mana village is that way.'

'Yes I know…' I said 'But I want to go to Mana pass.'

'Sorry sir…you cannot go on this road without permission.'

'But I do have permission!' I said triumphantly, presenting the SDM letter to him. 'See this.'

But to my surprise, he was totally unmoved.

'Sorry sir.. But I cannot let you pass unless I have permission from my superiors.'

'Eh?' I was foxed. 'But…but…I have official permission from the government! See this letter… a copy is marked to the Army as well.'

But he was unmoved. 'No dude - no can do. I won't let you go unless you have permission from the Army.'

'But what about this SDM letter?' I demanded.

He was too polite to tell me that I could wipe my ass with that SDM letter as far he was concerned - but that was what he clearly meant.

Shit!

'C'mon man…' I pleaded with him. 'I spent a whole day running around to get this letter yesterday. Don't do this to me…'

He felt sorry for me, and unbent a bit. 'Actually sir, you needed to get this stamped from the Army office at Joshimath for it to be valid for me. Then they would have called me and left instructions for me with details of travellers - names, registration numbers, ID numbers and all that - and then I would have checked your ID against my order and then you would have been allowed. That is the proper procedure.'

I sagged on my bike. Oh no. Going back to Joshimath and finding the concerned person and battling my way through Army bureaucracy to get the stamp would take a full day by itself.

'Isn't there any way I can get it stamped here at Badrinath?' I asked - but he just shook his head sorrowfully at me. He clearly sympathised with me - most people like solo bikers - but he was not going to go against his orders.

I heard that amused snicker again in my head. 'First things first, eh?' Badrinath was laughing at me.

'Oh all right... I am sorry... I am coming, I am coming.' I muttered.
'What was that?' the surprised soldier said.
'Nothing nothing... er...I ...let me try something...I will be back.'
'OK - but remember that unless I get a direct order on this phone here I cannot let you through.'

Chastened, I went back to Badrinath to pay my respects. This has happened to me multiple times...if we try to sneak past a deity without dropping in to pay my respects, I get a whack!

We tried to avoid meeting Tanglangla Pass in Ladakh by bypassing it with the Tso Moriri road - and the god of Tanglangla pass made us take a wrong turn - he actually pulled us back to ensure that we meet him and pay our respects. (Three Men on Motorcycles)
Delzad is still convinced that he had his accident in

Rajasthan because he refused to climb up to see the Osian devi temple (Three Men Ride Again)

Bharathi and her cycling friends tried to ride past the Krishna Temple at Ambalapuzha without dropping in during her cycling trip and she came down with a severe attack of the runs, which immediately went away after they all visited the temple.

I missed visiting the Mookambika temple in Karnataka because it was closed for siesta when I visited and I did not want to wait for it to reopen so I left without seeing - and immediately my bike broke down in the middle of the jungle and I spent the whole day getting it fixed. (Three Men Ride South)

After that we made it a point to go and visit any god that calls!

So I was convinced that the problem would go away once I went to Badrinath and paid my respects. I went to the temple and parked in front of that same dhaba and they were very happy to see me again!

'Arre! You are back? Where is your friend from Kerala?' - they were quite disappointed when I told them that George had gone back - they had liked him.

I called my brother and told him my sad tale, and he told me that I was a complete fool to not get the letter stamped from the Army - but now he would see what could be done.

With that part put in action, I decided to go and visit Badrinath and pay my most humble respects.

I was too lazy to take off my riding gear, so I clumped to the temple in riding gear. I entered the main temple - but there was a bit of a line to get into the inner sanctum sanctorum of the temple, and I had no enthu to get into that line - so I just did a genuflection from the main entrance and then sat inside the temple courtyard, waiting for the phone call from the Army.

Bro called after some time and said that the issue is trickling down the chain of command and someone from the Army will call me to take it up. I thanked him - if not for his help, nothing would have happened here. Soon I got a call from a Major Mumbledname of the Army, who seemed to be convinced that I was off my onion!

'Dude - the road is insanely screwed! Why would you want to go there? And that too alone? No no no…it is not safe for a solo rider to go all the way to the pass!'

'Ok ok…' I had been expecting that response. The point was very valid - if I fell or got stuck or got a breakdown somewhere, then they would be stuck with the job of helping me out. And to be honest, my bike was not in great shape and it was not the brightest of ideas to stress it so much.

But having come so far and taken so much effort, I wanted desperately to do at least some section of this road. 'Let's drop the idea of going all the way to Mana pass - can I at least go to Ghastoli village? That's just a few kilometres inside the road and I will at least get a flavour of the road.'

* * *

Major Mumbledname was caught wrong-footed! He had come on the line all set to refuse me permission to go to Mana pass and had prepared all sorts of detailed logical arguments in his head- and my change of tactic confused him utterly. There was no logical reason to refuse this request!

'Er...um...let me check and call you back on that...' he said, and hung up.

I pursed my lips and looked at Badrinath again. Clearly my visit had assuaged him somewhat, but he was still a bit huffed that I had not made the full effort and not done everything by the book.

OK OK - I said - Have it your way. I went outside, stripped off all my riding gear and clothes and entered the holy hot water spring - the Tapta Kund - and had a long dip in the sulphurous waters. It was most relaxing, and a great peace came over me… bodily and mental relaxation. I could feel the tension evaporating and my desires getting less intense.

What will be, will be… I will go to Mana pass if Badri wills it…I will not go if he does not. What does it matter?

The important thing is to achieve inner peace - be calm and cheerfully accept what is given to you.

I came out of the kund and again went to the temple - and this time the queue had magically disappeared! I was able to just walk in to the sanctum and have a lovely 'darshan' of the idol - and a communion with the deity. I suddenly realised that I am missing out on the actual spiritual experience of visiting Badrinath - I should be opening my mind and just soaking in the atmosphere of the place.

I came out of the sanctum and just chilled in the temple area - my body relaxed from the hot bath and my mind relaxed from my sudden giving up of desire. I quietly sat around observing the visitors and pilgrims… here there were a bunch of dudes from South India, shivering a bit in their lungis, there there was a lady all decked up in flowers and was singing devotional songs… singing them very badly, to be sure - but hey, let's hope that her heart was pure though her voice was cracked.

At one of the junior temples, I saw a hyper-enthusiastic priest who was conducting a prayer with full vigour - reciting the shlokas with full passion and ringing his little bell and almost weeping with rapture. The pandit's joy was a sight to behold when a pilgrim came up and also started loudly reciting the shlokas along with him! He was almost vibrating with excitement and was as happy as a eager puppy who has been whistled at by his master! His face lit up like a light bulb, his volume went even higher and his bell started ringing even louder - he wriggled all over as if he was frantically waving an invisible tail!

That show of enthusiastic devotion really cheered me up! Most people are rather serious and lugubrious in a temple, and the sight of much joy was wonderful.

My phone rang - it was Major Mumbledname again. This time he was not able to find a logical reason to say 'No' to me - so he told me to find the local ITBP commandant and take his permission. If I was able to get that guy's permission in writing, then he would allow me to enter the Mana pass road.

I laughed out aloud. This was like a fairy tale - where the prince is told to get the feather of a magical parrot from a island across the sea, or something like that. It might have been a polite way to tell me to buzz off - and if not my newly engendered peace of mind, I might have got discouraged and done just that. But now I just smiled and said - OK, let me try.

I again arrayed myself with my riding gear and put on my helmet, feeling like a knight going on a mythical quest.

I went hunting for the ITBP base - the soldiers there had come to know of me by now, and I think they were impressed by my dedication and were rooting for me! They enthusiastically pointed out the way to ITBP base and I rode over there, much to the sentry's confusion. I demanded to see the Commandant - and when they heard of my strange request, I was passed around from officer to mystified officer like a hot potato - until finally a senior looking guy with an impressive amount of brassware on his shoulders came to be and said that they dont give permission to enter the pass - I would have to get permission from the SDM and the Army.

'Ha!' I said - pointing a finger at him 'Hold hard there! Dont move!'

'Eh?'

'Don't move a muscle!' I cried, and pulled out my phone and called Major Mumbledname and made him talk to the ITBP guy directly.

'Hello..Deputy Commandant Mugwump here...eh? What?... No...why should I care?...he has SDM permission, he has your permission...where do I enter the picture? ... No no... it's your call entirely...' He shrugged and handed the phone back to me.

Poor Major Mumbledname had run out of excuses to say 'No' - so he tried one last gambit... 'Actually I can't get in touch with guard at the gate...he is not picking up the phone...'

'Hold hard!' I cried 'Stay on the line!'

'Eh?'

'Stay on the line!' I said, as I leapt on the bike and rode at top speed to the gate and screeched to a halt in front of the startled guard, and handed him the phone! 'Talk to your boss, buddy!'

Finally the army acquiesced to my persistence and allowed me to enter.

'You will have to leave your phone and all cameras here!' the guard told me worriedly. 'No Go-pro, no phone, no dash cam ... no imaging device of any sort allowed.'

'You got it dude.' I said, handing over my phone.

(I always wonder about this anti-camera fetish of the security forces - especially on an open road. The Chinese must be having detailed satellite photos of every rock and pebble here...what will they need a little phone camera photo for? Let an innocent tourist make memories for himself. But who can argue with the military mind?)

So finally that gate swung open!

With the grace of Lord Badrinath, my brother, the SDM, Major Mumbledname, the ITBP gentleman and this guard here - I was finally on the road to Mana pass!

WOOHOO!

I WAS GOING WHERE NO SOLO RIDER HAD BEEN BEFORE!

I zoomed up a steep slope and suddenly I was facing a giant and powerful river!
Wow!
This was the mighty Saraswati!
What a rush to see this powerful river! Awesome. Rather than the Mana pass road, they should call it the Saraswati valley road. It was a wonderful sight… the word 'awesome' is very overused, and hence has lost it's original connotation…it means being awed…scared… - by the sight of something powerful and scary…that's where the word 'Awful' comes from too. This sight was truly 'Awesome'! The sheer power and menace of that roaring river was really something.

I wonder how it would have felt in ancient times to the travellers who travelled by this road to Mana pass and then on to Tibet. The Portuguese priest António de Andrade and Manuel Marques who were the first travellers to Tibet had taken this route - and I wondered how they felt on seeing this sight? Did they fall to their knees and pray? Did they feel that they are in the land of ancient and powerful gods?

The Army was constructing a big road - in a few years they will have a spanking new road here and big trucks will be able to roll up to Mana pass in a few hours. But as of now, it was a huge mess. A half-done road is much worse than a dirt track - rocks and stones and iron bars and concrete dust everywhere.

But the advantage was that the road was done in some places and so I could comfortably in patches - and every now and then I used to stop and gape open-mouthedly at the scenery. The scenery had changed as if I had flicked a switch! Suddenly I was in a dry and brown landscape - like Ladakh or Spiti! The mountain had abruptly changed from the gentle green Himalayas to the brown and sere Himalayan desert!

All around me was the earth-palette of browns and reds and blacks - and the sky was an impossible shade of blue - and the roaring white torrent of the Saraswati below provided a rumbling splashing background music to the thumping of my bike.

It was amazing!

I passed a number of road labourers who didn't even give me a second glance - but then I came face to face with a jeep full of soldiers -and the driver looked at me incredulously! He couldn't believe his eyes! What on earth was a solo rider doing on this road?

He screeched to a halt, and frantically waved me to a halt. I stopped and the jeep stopped, and a bunch of guys came out. The leader was a guy in civvies, but his severe hair style and his military mien made it clear that he was an Army guy.

* * *

He goggled at me in disbelief, and came slowly up to me. I took off my helmet immediately to show my honest and innocent face to them, and smiled winningly at them. A cheerful and confident smile is always a good first gambit - it shows that you are a nice guy, and also that you are not afraid of them and they should treat you respectfully. The Army guy took in my Maharashtra registration number plate and was even more taken aback.

'How did you come here?' he asked me. 'This is not allowed.'

I leapt at his accent - he was definitely a Maharashtrian! Ha!

'But I do have permission.' I told him in Marathi. 'I have permission from the SDM, the ITBP and your Major Mumbledname.'

The poor guy was totally gobsmacked on being addressed in Marathi. And my confident mention of three big names had taken the wind out of his sails.

'I...er....Who are you?' he asked finally.

'I am a tourist from Mumbai' I told him, and told him of my adventures in getting a permit to come here. The guy made a call to the guard on his wireless and confirmed my story, and then became quite friendly as his suspicions were eased. We chatted for a bit in Marathi, and I could see that he was quite happy to meet a fellow Maharashtrian so unexpectedly out here on the Mana pass road. He was from Satara in Maharashtra, and was posted here in Army intelligence, just as I had suspected, and he was in charge of security here - which explained his suspicious attitude. Any other guy would probably just have ignored me. But since my bona fides were proven, we parted on good terms and I continued on my way.

The scenery continued to be incredible and I rode on like I was in a trance. The transition from the green hills to the brown hills was spectacular, and memories of all my previous rides went through my mind as I rode here - Ladakh, Zanskar, Nubra valley, Shyok, Killar, Kishtawar etc. I was sad that Adi and Delzad were not with me to enjoy this sight - but the experience of experiencing this all alone was something else!

When you are alone, you see things differently - feel things differently. And this feeling should be enjoyed when it is fresh… after a few days of solo travel you get habituated to it, and the thrill goes away. It still remains fun, I am sure - but you probably lose the raw thrill of the first few days.

I rode along slowly - not that I had a choice, the road was in a fairly bad condition. But even if it had been as smooth as glass, I still would have gone slowly to enjoy this experience and soak in the scenery. I always try to have time to stand and stare.

But alas - the Ghastali post came up soon, and there was a sentry standing there waiting for me. He had put a barrier across the road to ensure that I did not sneak on ahead - but he had no need to fear. I had no intention of breaking any orders.

I greeted him and parked my bike on the side of the road.
'Thus far, and no further!' he announced dramatically.
'Yeah yeah, I know.' I said. 'Can I stand here for a bit and stretch my legs?'
He was OK with that, and even offered me a cup of tea and I shared some chocolates I was carrying, and we had a nice little break. He also must have appreciated the little variety in his

rather dull routine.

'It's a good thing you are not going any further.' He confided to me. 'The river has flooded its banks further on and even our big trucks are having trouble crossing it.'

It was a bit sad that I could not complete the trip to Mana pass - but I was happy with this small ride to Ghastali. And as I mentioned earlier - it really was not safe for a solo rider to be doing this kind of terrain...and that too on a bike with issues - My chain was grumbling again. I was happy with what Badri had given.

I turned back and the ride back was even more enjoyable - because I was facing the river, and I came down marvelling at the scenery and the glory of the Saraswati. There was a ferocious waterfall at one point - and the entire river vanished underground for a bit! I stood there - astonished, looking at the view.

An army guard was standing there morosely, no doubt wondering what I was doing here in the middle of nowhere when I could have been comfortably at home having a drink and eating pakoras, as he was probably fantasising about.

He saw me staring at the river, and told me that it was very dangerous! A big army truck had fallen into it and had completely vanished! It was never seen again!

I came to the top of that first slope I had climbed - and stopped the bike and got off! What a view!

The entire Badrinath valley lay spread out before me! I could see the silvery strands of the Alaknanda mixing with the shining Saraswati just beyond Mana village and the wide green valley of

Badrinath. I could clearly make out the brightly coloured Badrinath temple, surrounded by the chaos of the pilgrim town. I could see the Army camp, the ITBP camp and the ancient Mana village. There was Bhimpul…and there was the road to the falls…

Imagine seeing this sight in the olden days, when the temple might be the only structure to be seen! Think of what must have gone through the mind of the Tibetan traveller as he emerged from the brown wastes of the high deserts and saw this lovely green valley for the first time. And to think that this whole valley is covered with snow in the winters! Wow!

I stood there for a long time, just watching that scene.

I wonder what that young Keralite boy called Shankaracharya must have thought when he climbed to this place so many centuries ago. 'I must set up a Matha here' he must have thought. 'For the glory of God.'

I sighed and got on my bike again. My Mana pass ride adventure was over.

I came down to the gate - much to the sentry's relief. I thanked him and collected my phone and left.

I had a tea outside the Badrinath area and went down slowly back to Joshimath.

I rode as slowly as possible, trying to soak up the views and memories - like a camel drinking at an oasis.

What a wonderful day… Badrinath and Mana.

* * *

Jai Badri Vishal!

Malari and Niti valley

Another day full of adventure!

But where to go? I had earlier planned to go to Gangotri and explore the Nilang valley there - but then I would spend a whole day getting there and would not have time to explore the Gangotri area in a leisurely manner. I decided to drop Gangotri from this trip and make another trip to explore that part of Uttarakhand - that would enable to explore the Joshimath area today…and have a brilliant reason to return to the mountains for a second visit!

I decided instead to go and check out the famous Niti pass -

another border area with Tibet.

Obviously I would not be able to go all the way to Niti - more's the pity. But the thought of again going through all that process for getting a pass to see Niti pass gave me a pain in the neck. And anyway, that SDM would probably throw me out and Major Mumbledname might send some soldiers to kick my butt if I went asking for more permissions.

And of course, the issue with my bike and it's rattly chain...

But hey! Let's go as far as I can. 'Excelsior'!

The shades of night were falling fast,

As through an Alpine village passed
A youth, who bore, 'mid snow and ice,
A banner with the strange device,
    Excelsior!

I geared up and left my good Joshimath hotel for the last time and again got on that same Auli road. I passed by all the Army and sundry Amry-esque establishments and got on the road to Niti pass.

It was a phenomenal road climbing up to Auli and then riding down the slope and I stopped several times to take in the scenery!

I was just admiring the road and scenery - when suddenly I was in the midst of road-building chaos! Broken roads, traffic mess, earthmoving equipment, tar-coated labourers and clouds of choking dust! Bloody hell!

It's a curse, I tell you! Wherever I go, whenever I go - there is somebody digging up the roads there!

I cursed a good bit and fought my way through it and found myself at the village of Tapovan - or 'Topobon' as some Bengali dude seemed to have named it as on Google Maps. The word 'Tapovan' comes from the two root words - tapas - meaning penance and by extension religious mortification and austerity, and more generally spiritual practice, and vana, meaning forest or thicket. Tapovan then translates as forest of austerities or spiritual practice.

Traditionally in India, any place where someone has engaged in serious spiritual retreat may become known as a tapovan, even if there is no forest. As well as particular caves and other hermitages where sages and sadhus have dwelt, there are some places, such as the western bank of the northern Ganges river around Rishikesh, that have been so used by hermits that the whole area has become known as a tapovan. There is a Tapovan in Nasik, one in Haridwar…and no doubt, numerous ones all over the country.

This particular 'Topobon' was in fact a hot spring! I was interested! I am always open to taking a refreshing dip in a hot spring! But when I asked locals, they pointed out a building pretty far away on the banks of the river - and anyway it was closed for some reason….might have been for repairs, or maybe for a siesta!

Anyway - Focus! The aim today is Malari and not to jump into hot water pools! En Avant! I put the bike in gear and roared off.

The Road goes ever on and on
Down from the door where it began.
Now far ahead the Road has gone,
And I must follow, if I can,
Pursuing it with eager feet,
Until it joins some larger way
Where many paths and errands meet.
And whither then? I cannot say.

- Tolkein

I was in the Dhauliganga valley now - and it was a wonderful sight! The Dhauliganga is a tributary of the Alaknanda, and it is a magnificent sight as it flows down from the Himalayan heights.

* * *

They are out to dam this river too! The Tapovan Vishnugad
Hydropower Plant is being constructed on Dhauliganga River -
and I am sure that it will fuck up the place entirely. Poor
Dhauliganga. Bloody environmental vandals.

But the river still looked awesome - and traffic thinned out
significantly after I crossed Tapovan and I would ride in a
relaxed manner and chill and enjoy the spectacular views of that
Dhauliganga valley - or the 'Niti valley' as it is called, after Niti -
the last village on the Indo-Tibetan border. This was also a
trading route for Indo-Tibet trade which was shut by China after
their Tibet heist and the Indo-China war of 1962.

I could see the massive peaks of the Nandadevi range, and
one of them was the peak of Dunagiri - a 7000 meter mountain
which was part of the ring of peaks surrounding the mighty
Nandadevi and enclosing the Nandadevi sanctuary. It was first
climbed in 1939 by a couple of Swiss climbers and was part of
the great mountaineering revolution of India of the early 1900s.

However, it is famous for a more more ancient and fun
reason! 'Dunagiri' is a corruption of 'Dronagiri' - and is
supposed to be extremely rich in medicinal herbs. The story
goes back to the ancient Hindu epic Ramayana. Rama - an
incarnation of Lord Vishnu - and his brother Lakshmana were
engaged in a war with the demon king Ravana in sri Lanka
(very long story…do check it out if you have not read it already)
Ravana's son - Indrajeet - unleashed a super-potent weapon
on Rama, but Lakshman leapt up to intercept it and it hit him
instead. This obviously knocked him for a six, and he was at
death's door. The doctor examined him, tapped his teeth
thoughtfully and said that the only thing that could save him

was a magical herb called 'Sanjeevani' - which could be found only on this Dronagiri mountain.

Maybe this was just a tactic by the doctor to tell Rama that Lakshman would not make it - but he was overtrumped by Hanuman, the magical monkey demi-god. He said that he could use his magical powers to fly all the way from Lanka to Uttarakhand...but how would he know which plant to pick?

The doctor gave him a detailed description - and Hanuman set out on his magical journey!

(Interestingly....it's on the same longitude!)

* * *

But when he reached there (more than a 1000 miles), identified the peak (from a whole bunch of identical looking mountains) and landed on it...he had completely forgotten what the bloody plant looked like!

Rather than go back and rather shamefacedly ask the doctor for a refresher on what it looked like - and possibly forget again - he decided to uproot the whole bloody mountain and fly it 1000 miles down to Lanka!

So - a dude who has magical powers without any limit - still can suffer from bad memory!

He should be worshipped as a god of absent-minded people!

When I heard this story as a kid, I swallowed it whole...but now...hahaha...face palm! What a yarn.

Oh well...why ruin a perfectly good legend with facts and logic? All religious legends are absurd anyway...that's the whole charm of it. Rains of frogs, parting of the sea, turning water into oil, talking animals, turning bread into fish, people rising from the dead, people being carried to heaven on flying horses, etc. If it was not patently impossible … what would be godly and miraculous about doing it?

But I do hope Hanuman came and put the mountain back! Did Rama say to him 'A place for everything, and everything in its place'?

To my great joy, there was actually a sign pointing to the mountain, and saying 'Hanuman lifted Dronagiri here'.

I practically leapt off my bike to emulate his feat myself!

Now that one thinks of it, the act of ripping up an entire

mountain by the roots and carrying it a 1000 miles away - when you just needed a few leaves of a certain plant - smacks of rampant environmental vandalism! It shows the disregard plains people have for the ecology of the mountains, even in ancient legends!

And rather suitably, this valley is also the home of the first people's environment movement where the local people banded together and protested to save their environment from the depredations of the plains people - the CHIPKO movement.

The word 'Chipko' literally means to 'Stick to the tree' and it literally meant that village women hugged the trees and refused to let the loggers cut the trees! If they wanted to cut the trees, then they would have to cut through their bodies first!

The whole story reflects most unfavourably on the local government mechanism - especially bad considering that it was a time of newly independent India where people's rights should have been treated with more respect! The local government machinery was extremely corrupt and insensitive and sold mining and logging rights in these ecologically fragile mountains to bribe-giving outsiders, who stripped the country bare and left the place a ruin.

The contractors brought in their own men from the plains and cut down all the trees and blasted the mountains for limestone - and caused monumental environmental damage, resulting in the devastating Alaknanda River floods of July 1970, when a major landslide blocked the river and affected an area starting from Hanumanchatti, near Badrinath to 320 kilometers downstream till Haridwar, further numerous villages, bridges and roads were washed away. Thereafter, incidences of

landslides and land subsidence became common in an area
which was experiencing a rapid increase in civil engineering
projects.

The forest department was completely culpable in this,
disregarding the needs and wishes of the locals and recklessly
awarding huge logging contracts to outsiders. Numerous
protests and demonstrations and letters had no impact on the
babus, until finally there was a standoff in 1972 and 73 where
loud and strident protests from locals deterred a few logging
contracts.
But the Government guys were shameless, and in 1974 they
announced an auction - a much bigger auction for 2500 trees as
opposed to a few hundred trees earlier - in Reni village in this
Dhauliganga valley.
The locals decided to protest with a tree-hugging movement to
protect the trees - and the government guys actually played
insanely dirty! They lied to the villagers that they will be paid a
compensation and sent them by truck to a fictitious address!
And while the villagers were still hunting for this fictional
compensation place, the contractors sent an army of loggers to
quickly cut the trees down! It would be a fait accompli! All the
protests in the world would be of no avail once the trees were
cut.

The sheer shamelessness and chutzpah of this was breath-
taking.

Luckily for the forests, a little girl saw the loggers driving up
and ran to alert Gaura Devi, the head of the village ladies
organisation. Gaura Devi led 27 of the village women to the site
and confronted the loggers. When all talking failed, and the
loggers started to shout and abuse the women, threatening them

with guns - the women resorted to hugging the trees to stop them from being felled. This went on into late hours. The women kept an all-night vigil guarding their trees from the cutters until a few of them relented and left the village. The next day, when the men and leaders returned, the news of the movement spread to the neighbouring areas, and more people joined in. Eventually, after a four-day stand-off, the contractors left.

The news soon reached the state capital, where the then state Chief Minister, Hemwati Nandan Bahuguna, set up a committee to look into the matter, which eventually ruled in favour of the villagers. This became a turning point in the history of eco-development struggles in the region and around the world..

On 26 March 2004, Reni, Laata, and other villages of the Niti Valley celebrated the 30th anniversary of the Chipko movement, where all the surviving original participants united. The celebrations started at Laata, the ancestral home of Gaura Devi, where Pushpa Devi, wife of late Chipko Leader Govind Singh Rawat, Dhoom Singh Negi, Chipko leader of Henwalghati, Tehri Garhwal, and others were celebrated. From here a procession went to Reni, the neighbouring village, where the actual Chipko action took place on 26 March 1974.

I wish I could say that the Chipko movement won - but the sheer amount of dam construction in all the hill states says otherwise. There was a huge dam coming up right there in Niti valley!

There were multiple cases of the Government saying 'Fuck you' and 'Too bad' and 'Can't make omelettes without breaking eggs' to local people, tribal and forest communities all over India. The huge Kedarnath floods of 2013 showed how bad the environmental situation is - but it seems to have been forgotten already. There is an orgy of dam building, mining, construction, road building through forests and all kinds of activities which totally fuck up the environment - with the full blessing of the central government.

Right now as I write this, the Union minister of Environment and the Minister of Heavy Industry is the same person - talk about a conflict of interest! A 'rubber-stamp' ministry indeed. Huge numbers of forests are being felled left and right, and ecology strained like never before.

But at least it showed a mirror to the money-hungry, eco-insensitive, bribe-hungry government posture - and succeeding governments at least had to pay lip-service to the the environment, and needs of local people. There are a number of environment protection laws in place now and there is intent - at least on paper - to save the environment.

But as of now the valley was still beautiful! The skies were blue, and the clouds were white and puffy and the roads were smooth and I sang in my helmet as I went down this valley.

I finally reached the village of Malari - and the end of the road! The army guys had put a bar across the road and access beyond that was only for locals, armed forces people and permit-holders.

I did not have a permit, and didn't even attempt to argue. I was happy at whatever ride I was able to have! It had been a magical journey.

* * *

I asked the guards where I could get something to eat and they pointed me to the residential area of the ITBP. There was a canteen there which was open to civilians. I went there and it was nice cozy little place where I enjoyed a bun-omelette and a chai.

Well that was it for Niti pass. A shame I couldn't get to the end of the road - maybe some other time!

I turned back and rode slowly back, embracing the views of the Niti valley and the glorious Dhauliganga.

As I reached Joshimath, I sighed. What a glorious day! It was a shame to leave this beautiful area!

I looked up to see that bright blue sky again - and I was shocked to see dark black stormclouds rapidly talking over half the sky!

Oh shit! Rain!

I made a run for it!. I had a long steep and curvy descent down from Joshimath and I had no desire to do it in the rain. Apart from being freezing cold, it would make the roads wet, muddy and slippery and reduce my speed considerably.

I zoomed down the twisty roads, outrunning the rain.

What a rush that was! I really enjoyed that swift ride down. I was enjoying going down that curvy road and bending the bike steeply and trying to scrape my footpegs and was keeping an eye on the dark clouds in my rear view mirror.

I went ZIP ZAP ZOOM and was almost all the way down

before the rains overtook me. I could feel the rain come up - the temperature came down and the humidity increased and I could just feel the rain about to form! I was on the lookout for a nice covered hotel - and I was lucky enough to find one just as the rain hit! I parked the bike inside and looked with satisfaction at the rain pouring down. What fun it is to be indoors when it's raining outdoors.

I enjoyed a hot Maggi noodles and a chai and waited out the shower and then continued on my journey.

My route now was to go down to Baniyakund - I would get off this rather crowded highway at Gopeshwar and take a smaller state road which would be lovely and peaceful and less infested with trucks.

I was most happy to take the turnoff and the road became much quieter - and unfortunately this meant that I could hear my poor chain rattling and groaning away!

Oh no - not again!

Luckily there was a mechanic shop right there and I pulled up.
The mechanic just shrugged and said the only thing he could do
was to oil the chain. And this did indeed reduce the rattling
considerably - but I knew that this was only a temporary fix.
But at least the most challenging part of the ride was over - I
would be riding in fairly low altitude now and half the ride was
done.

Just pray to the lord of motorbike travel and hope that the bike
survives the next few days.

The roads after the turnoff were an absolute delight! What
lovely views! What empty and peaceful roads! What lovely
sinuous curves! What forests! What trees!

What incomparable air!

I love the word 'Petrichor' which describes this smell …'Petra'
+ 'ichor' - literally the 'lifeblood of the earth'.

Interestingly, I could feel that the petrichor of the mountains
and forests is different from the petrichor of the plains!
The air in the mountains after the rains is something to be felt. It
is fresh and clean and smells of all the good things in the
world… of the wet rocks, of the green trees, of the sap, of the
flowers, of the insects, of the wet tar of the road, of the steam
forming when the cold rain hits the hot tar roads…

It was a joy to be riding on this road.

* * *

But then, the fun of rain in the mountains is best felt when you are indoors, and not while you are getting wet in the rains. I kept a lookout on the sky and I could feel another build up of rain coming up.

And it was getting on to evening as well, and I didn't fancy the idea of being wet and cold in the night. The roads had been strangely deserted and hotel-free till now and I was getting rather nervous, and the rain was almost on me - and I magically found a hotel just in the nick of time!

I stopped at the hotel and spoke to the proprietor. I wondered whether to press on - but then I looked at the sky and said - fuck it, I will stay here.

And talk about a perfectly-timed decision! No sooner had I taken the bags of my bike that it started pouring!

I was so happy! YES! WHAT TIMING! WOO HOO!

I settled down happily in the hotel and had a nice hot bath and enjoyed a relaxing rum and water before tucking into a virtuous freshly cooked vegetarian dinner - a complete spread of dal, sabji, chawal and fresh hot chapatis.

Ah what a lovely day!

Good bye Badrinath and Joshimath. It was great seeing you.

Tungnath

The next morning I got up at dawn, and jumped out of bed! It was going to be another awesome day! WOOHOO

I heard the chirping of birds outside my window and looked out to see a lovely dawn scene. The rain clouds had expended themselves and the morning looked clean and bright. The rain had cleaned up the air and washed all the suspended particles away and the mountains looked clean and green and inviting.

I thought that I would go out to take in that incomparable mountain air - but when I went to front gate, I found it securely shuttered and locked! The safety-conscious owner had drawn the shutter and locked it with a sturdy lock - either to keep thieves out, or to prevent sly guests from leaving without paying their bills.

Oh well…so much for the incomparable morning air. I sniffed at it through the bars and then went back to my room. In earlier times it used to be a big pain to sit around and wait for the wait-staff to wake up and get to work before you could get your cup of tea - but now! Aha! I had my trusty little water-heater and packs of powdered tea. I could now treat the foibles of the sleepy stuff with a light laugh as I made myself a cup of awesome tea. Girnar instant tea - you rock!

I enjoyed that cup of tea so much that I made myself another cup of tea and looked at the mountains.

'Through the open window, I focus on a pattern of small,

glossy lime leaves; then through them I see the mountains, the Himalayas, striding away into an immensity of sky.

"In a thousand ages of the gods I could not tell thee of the glories of Himachal". So confessed a Sanskrit poet at the dawn of Indian history and he came closer than anyone else to capturing the spell of the Himalayas. The sea has had Conrad and Stevenson and Masefield, but the mountains continue to defy the written word. We have climbed their highest peaks and crossed their most difficult passes, but still they keep their secrets and their reserve; they remain remote, mysterious, spirit-haunted.'

- Ruskin Bond

Satisfied and content with my tea and the pleasant philosophising, I bathed and packed up and was ready to leave by the time the hotel-staff woke up and fed me breakfast.

Last night I had curiously asked the hotel guy why there were two hotels here next to each other, while there were no hotels at all all the way from Gopeshwar to here - and he replied that this was the start of the trekking trail to Rudranath and hence there was good business from the various trekking groups.

Rudranath! I was immediately interested! Rudranth was part of the 'Panch Kedar' or 'Five Kedars' - ancient temples of Shiva. The chief of these was Kedarnath - which I had already trekked to once (One Man Gets the Sack), and the others were Tungnath, Rudranath, Madhyamaheshwar and Kalpeshwar.

'How long does it take to trek from here?' I asked eagerly - but immediately subsided when he said 'three days. It is quite a tough trek for you fat...er...plains people'. I did not have three days to spare… I would have to make another trip to Uttarakhand for that. Actually, I would have to make many many trips. There was so much to see and do here.

And suddenly the urge to do another trek flamed up inside me!

It was not on the plan at all - but I suddenly decided to trek to Tungnath.

But you are alone…on a bike… my logical mind said to me worriedly.

So?

What do you mean, 'So'? Who will take care of your bike? How will you trek in your riding gear? Where will you stow that? What if someone steals all your stuff and goes, eh? What will you do then?

Tchah. Pah. I waved my logical mind's objections aside. I will just find a dhaba and become his customer and ask him to watch my bike and gear.

But…but…you are alone. And fat. And unfit…. Logical mind said worriedly. Will you be able to do such a steep climb? What if you are not able to make it? What if you fall and get injured? How will you ride the bike then?

Tchah. Bah. I may be fat - but I am not unfit! Didn't I do the Valley of flowers trek just now? I will make it - never fear! Mind over matter and all that!

* * *

But …but…

Oh shut up! And bugger off! I bellowed - and my logical mind got offended!

There is no need to be offensive, it said coldly. I was just trying to look out for you.

Sorry dude.. But there is a time for logic and there is a time for LUNACY! BUAHAHAHA!

I looked up from my internal conflict and saw the hotel guy looking at me in an alarmed manner and backing away! Ooops….did I say that out loud?

I quickly got on my bike and roared away - leaving the most relieved hotel guy behind.

* * *

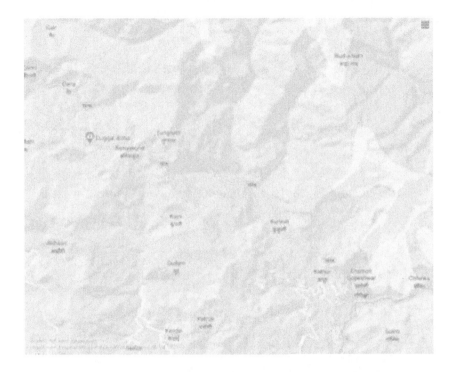

As I rode on that road… (wow, that's poetry) … I realised what a wise decision it had been to stay in that hotel yesterday! Not only was the hotel a lovely place - reasonably priced, lovely scenery and good food - but it was the only hotel around! If I had gone on ahead, then I would have been stuck cold and wet in miles and miles of dense jungle.

(Not that I made a conscious decision… it was the Patron saint of Idiots who protects me. All I do is take the most conservative path and try not to ride after dark.)

And why should you ride after dark? You are doing the ride to see the country after all - why ride if you cannot see the country?

And was this country worth seeing! Wow! The road entered a

jungle soon after the hotel - and much to my most pleasant surprise, it turned out that I was in a wildlife sanctuary! I saw a sign that told me that I was in the 'Kedarnath musk deer sanctuary' - a place that I hadn't even heard of.

The views were simply spectacular! I was riding on a high ridge and a whole vista of scenery was laid out in front of me. The mountains were green and forested, and there was still a bank of clouds tarrying in the midst of the mountains. The green terraces of the farmed fields lay in pleasant ripples where the industrious farmers were growing rice and all sort of delicious veggies, I suppose - and the blue-black slate roofs of the village houses stuck out here and there, giving a most pleasing shire-like look.

Deep in the crouching mist, lie the mountains.
Climbing the mountains are forests
Of rhododendron, spruce and deodar—
Trees of God, we call them—soughing

In the wind from the passes of Garhwal;
And the snow-leopard moans softly
When the herdsmen pass, their lean sheep cropping
Short winter grass.
And clinging to the sides of the mountains,
The small stone houses of Garhwal

- Ruskin Bond

The roads through the sanctuary were ab-so-lute-ly magical… it was like a little patch of heaven - and all the more pleasing because it was so completely unexpected! Neither the hotel guy nor Google maps had told me about it and so it was an unexpected treat.

The roads were small and twisty and almost entirely deserted, and I felt that I had the whole jungle to myself. The forest was pretty dense and seemed to be a genuine old forest and not a replanted one - from the variety of trees. Small streams flowed here and there, and there were birds fluttering about - no doubt glaring at my bike for disturbing that primordial peace.

The place was an absolute joy for a solo rider - there were no other vehicles to disturb the peace and I could ride as slowly as I pleased and make frequent stops to adore that forest and its stillness. I went along as slowly as I could - because I wanted to slowly enjoy this road the way I would eat slowly to enjoy a wonderful meal. What a treat for the senses!

I was hoping to catch a sight of the musk deer for whom the sanctuary was made - but no luck there. These deer look strangely ferocious and vampire-like - having 'fangs' instead of antlers, but are extremely shy and the noise of the rumbly bike would have scared them away.

The musk deer or 'kasturi' as they are called in Hindi, are so named for the waxy substance called 'musk' that the male secretes from a gland in the abdomen. The deer use this to mark territories and attract females.
The smell of its own musk can apparently madden the deer with lust - and this has been used as an example by various Indian mystics to describe the human condition - being maddened by the want of something which is actually resident within

yourself.

'Kasturi kundal base, mrag dhundhat ban mahi
Jaise ghat ghat ram hai, duniya dekhe nahi'

'A deer has the fragrance within itself, but runs throughout the forest in search of it...
Similarly, the Lord is everywhere, but the world does not perceive him'

- Saint Kabir

This musk has unfortunately been the cause of other problems for the deer - humans use this musk to make perfumes and that unfortunate stag has been hunted almost to extinction to attain that bag of musk - hence the need for a musk deer sanctuary.

At every beautiful spot I would stop and switch off the engine and just sit quietly for a few minutes to listen to the forest... the breeze, the rustling of the leaves, the gurgling of a little brook, the drip drip of raindrops, the twittering and fluttering of the birds, the soft crunch of some animal hiding in the woods, the plink plink of my exhaust as it cooled down, the sound of my own breath inside my helmet...

Then I would shake myself and smile and start my bike - and that joyful roar was wonderful too!

Life is good.

The road went steadily uphill through the forest - and suddenly I came to an open ridge and gasped at the awesome views of snow-capped mountains!

Gosh and Golly! Where did these guys come from?!!

* * *

WOW!

I was lost in wonder, and was most pleased when I came across a nest of tea stalls in the jungle. Actually I passed them by first, because I was in a hurry to get to Tungnath - then I realised that the sanctuary is getting over and it would be a shame to leave this place so soon... so I turned back!

Thats the fun of being alone... you can do as you please.

I enjoyed a couple of cups of hot tea, soaking in the last views of the sanctuary and the first views of the mountains. A passing motorist was amazed to see my MH Maharashtra registration and stopped to have a chat with this crazy guy who has come so far on a motorcycle.

And soon - sadly - the sanctuary was done, and I was back on the main road. It was a good thing that I had been on those roads so early and hence enjoyed the silence and solitude of the ride. Now I could see a number of vehicles on the road.

And within a few minutes I was at Tungnath!

There was no village as such - just a small and rather inconspicuous arch announcing the start of the trail and a small collection of modest dhabas. I parked my bike in front of one and asked him if he would watch my bike and stuff, and stuffed myself with some awesome parathas to fuel myself for the climb ahead. I went into his back room and stripped off my riding gear and changed into trekking gear and set out!

Tungnath baba was calling me! There was no other explanation for this sudden urge of mine.

When I reached the starting point, all the horse and pony-wala's jumped up with joy at seeing me!

This fat old fuck could not be expected to climb Tungnath on his own! I was most surely a customer.

Tchah! Pah! Gah! I waved them all away imperiously.

What do you think I am? I shall climb alone and unassisted!
* * *

I started up that path, huffing and puffing. It was pretty steep and I used my usual technique of walking for 500 meters and taking a breather, and then walking …and repeat. The advantage of doing this alone was there was no one to match pace with - no one to catch up to - and no one to wait for. I could set my own pace and be comfortable.

Do this tortoise and hare stuff, and you will be surprised at what you can achieve! Soon I saw that I had gained quite a bit of height, and the views were absolutely magnificent! The air was amazingly clear, and the visibility was awesome… the whole Chaukhamba range was visible in front of me in all its glory.

* * *

To my amusement, I saw the sign for a college there - The High altitude plant physiology research centre, of the the H N Bahuguna Garhwal university!

These students must be really fit, I thought… not to mention the teachers as well!

* * *

'The mountains and valleys of Garhwal never fail to spring surprises on the traveller in search of the picturesque. It is impossible to know every corner of the Himalayas, which means that there are always new corners to discover; forest or meadow, mountain stream or wayside shrine.

The temple of Tungnath, at a little over 12,000 feet, is the highest shrine on the inner Himalayan range. It lies just below the Chandrashila peak. Some way off the main pilgrim routes, it is less frequented than Kedarnath or Badrinath, although it forms a part of the Kedar temple establishment. The priest here is a local man, a Brahmin from the village of Maku; the other Kedar temples have South Indian priests, a tradition begun by Sankaracharya, the eighth-century Hindu reformer and revivalist.

Tungnath's lonely eminence gives it a magic of its own. To get there (or beyond it), one passes through some of the most delightful temperate forest in the Garhwal Himalayas. Pilgrim or trekker, or just plain rambler like myself, one comes away a

Ketan Joshi

better man, forest-refreshed and more aware of what the world was really like before mankind began to strip it bare.

The trek from Chopta to Tungnath is only three and a half miles, but in that distance one ascends about 3000 feet, and the pilgrim may be forgiven for feeling that at places he is on a perpendicular path. 'Like a ladder to heaven,' I couldn't help thinking.'

- Ruskin Bond

A ladder to heaven indeed! The last climb up to the temple was so steep that I was huffing and puffing like a blacksmith's bellows by the time I reached there!

And no wonder - Tungnath is one of the highest Shiva temples in India - even higher than Kedarnath temple...being at 3680 mts, as compared to 3583 mts of Kedarnath.
It is the highest of the Panch Kedars - though of course, the road is much nearer to the top than the others. It takes a full day to reach Kedar from Gaurikund, and 3 days to reach Rudranath - while it takes only a few hours to reach here.

The Panch Kedar temples are linked to the stories of the Pandavas - you remember I spoke about them earlier during the Mana village chapter. The fratricidal Pandavas were trying to expiate their sins and wanted to catch Lord Shiva and beg his forgiveness. Shiva did not want to meet them and tried to avoid them by changing his shape into that of a bull and mixing with other cattle - but the Pandavas spotted him and came chasing after him.
Shiva must have muttered 'Oh no! Not them again' - and tried to sink into the ground, and almost succeeded too - but his hump was still above ground and Bheema caught hold of that and refused to let it go underground. Shiva was pleased with their persistence (or sick of them) and materialised in front of

them and blessed them.

(This whole story is a very weird if you look at it with the cold eye of logic - the lord turns into a bull which sinks sloooowly into the ground in order to avoid meeting people... why a bull? Why not turn into a bird and fly away? Why not just vanish? If you are a bull...why sink into the ground? And that too so slowly that a big lumbering aged muscleman has enough time to dive and catch the hump? And so what if he catches hold of the hump? A hump is smooth and slippery and it would have slipped out of the grip if it had continued sinking into the ground? And so on and so forth.

But the whole point of these tales is suspension of logic I suppose. Poking holes in them ruins the fun , just like poking holes in superhero powers and origin stories. So we shall eschew logic!)

The Shiva representation at Kedarnath is a rock in the shape of that hump which Bheema caught hold of, and these other five temples are to commemorate sundry other parts of that bull - Tungnath is identified as the place where the bahu (hands) were seen (Wouldn't a bull have legs and not arms? Or are we talking about the human version?); head appeared at Rudranath; his navel and stomach (?) surfaced at Madhyamaheshwar; and his jata (matted locks of hair...like dreadlocks) at Kalpeshwar. (Again...the bull won't have matted locks...ah, forget it!)

This story is a lot of bull! But then - faith and legends are beyond logic and reason. It's like analysing a dew-drop... takes away the whole romance and feeling of it.

The temple was a very simple and ancient stone affair - and luckily had not been 'restored' or 'repaired' and hence maintained its ancient timeless charm. I rested for a while outside the temple to get my breath back, and then took off my shoes and went inside.

* * *

The utter simplicity of the place was heart-warming. The lingam was not a polished and artificial thing - but just a simple natural misshapen piece of rock. There were a few ancient sculptures, which apparently were renditions of the Adi Shankaracharya and symbols of the other Panch Kedars. There was an aura of peace and spirituality in the place which was very soothing.

I decided to do a pradakshina - a holy circumambulation - of the temple, and after having done that, I went and sat a little way from the temple. I thought about how Shiva is our 'kuldaivat' - our family deity, and how happy dad would have been to hear that I had been here. He had been to all the 'jyotirlingas' except for Kedarnath, and was very happy when I had been there.

And what happened there was exceedingly strange!

I was suddenly overcome by emotion! There was absolutely no reason for me to remember dad at that time, or to be so emotional about it… he had been gone for more than 10 years now - but it just happened out of the blue. It was a tidal wave of emotion!

I was totally overcome - and tears suddenly started flowing down my cheeks!

And before I knew it - I was sobbing! Sobbing bitterly! Like a child!

It was just amazing… I had never felt anything like this before. I sobbed and sobbed and tears flowed down my cheeks and I was snotty and blubbery.

I had never had just a visceral reaction to a place before. I don't think I have ever cried before - except when my mom died. But…I just couldn't control myself. I sat there crying and sobbing for quite some time before I was in control of myself again.

Emotions washed over me like waves on a beach - and just as gently, they went back... leaving behind a clean feeling, like the mountains after rain.

I sat there for several minutes, immersing myself in the spiritual power of that simple ancient temple.

What a feeling that was. I was deeply affected.

The emotional storm subsided and I was back to normal.

Whoa. What was that? What just happened?

I sat around for a bit - and realised that there was still a higher point than the temple - there was a trail going up somewhere. Intrigued, I also started walking up and found that this was the trail to Chandrashila peak - the summit of Tungnath, at 4000 meters (13000 feet) above sea level.

I huffed and puffed and toiled manfully up that slope - and it was more fun and more dangerous than the climb to the temple, because there was no stone path and no ladder and no railing of any sort. You had to scramble up and down rocks and slopes and stuff.

But finally I was at the peak! WOOHOO!

I WAS ON TOP OF TUNGNATH -CHANDRASHILA!

This peak is supposed to provide awesome views of the Himalayas, including Nandadevi, Trisul, Kedar Peak,

Bandarpunch and Chaukhamba peaks -

- but alas... by the time I got there, the clouds had gathered and there was nothing to be seen! It was just a blanket of white.

That's so sad! I was missing out on a wonderful view. Maybe if I had not tarried in the jungle, or at the temple I would have got a nice view.

But then, I might not - and then I would have missed those wonderful experiences in the jungle and the temple!

Life is like that.

I had noticed an elderly white-haired gentleman walking well in front of me on the trail and had used him as a model to motivate myself - if that white-haired old relic can do it, so can you! Move it you 'orrible little man! And keep moving! Leph Raaigh Leph... Leph Leph ...Leph Raaaigh Leph...

As such, I considered him a friend who had helped me climb up - and I was delighted to meet him on top of Chandrashila. It was a rather strange group of three people - this old gentleman, a young lady and a strapping local lad. Rather a strange ménage, I thought - but when I nodded and smiled at them and struck up a conversation with them I came to know that the local dude was a guide and these two were doing a trekking tour around the Panch Kedar.

The old dude and the lady were not together - they were just fellow customers of that trekking agent. The trek company provided a car, this guide and also organised food and accommodation and all logistics.

The elderly gentleman was a Gujarati - which added to the set of anomalies. Not many old people in India trek, very few Gujjus trek - and the intersection set was obviously even rarer. I was most admiring of his enthusiasm for life and shook his hand and congratulated him for doing a fairly difficult trek at his age.

And I realised that all three of them were almost equally surprised that I did this trek at my...er...weight. And when they learnt that I was alone and was doing a motorcycle tour around Uttarakhand by myself, they were quite impressed and became quite friendly.

As long as the old dude spoke hindi, I took him for a normal garden-variety gujju with an unusual taste in hobbies - but when he started speaking English, I was quite surprised to hear a strong American twang!

It turned out that he was actually an American citizen and genuine Potel ... a Motel-owning Patel. He had a motel in Florida - but came all the way to the Himalayas for his holidays. This guy was a rara avis indeed.

'Let's have a snack' he said at one point, and fished out a packet from his bag.
'What have you got there? Thepla?' I asked, laughing. All gujjus carry large packets of thepla with them wherever they go. It is a spiced flatbread, which tastes great and lasts forever - and so is a perfect travel food. You dont need to depend on dodgy outside food if you are carrying your fix of theplas. It was like a Gujju identification mark.
'Oh course thepla! What did you expect?' he replied laughing, and offered me one. I tasted it - and was struck by the distinct and unusual flavour.
'Oh, it's flavoured with Dill.' He said. 'We get nice Dill in Florida.'
I thought that it was a good representation of the man himself - a mix of Gujju and America, and therefore something quite unique.

The lady was a fellow Maharashtrian from Pune! We greeted

each other in Marathi and the others laughed to see our delight. She had left her husband behind and come alone to trek - he was not getting leave, and she very correctly decided that it was better to go alone than wait for him to get his holidays approved. I suppose the husband also would be equally happy and enjoying some relaxed quiet time at home.

We spent some time chatting on top, hoping for the clouds to clear so that we could get some of those famous views - but no joy there. Finally we made little cairns as a salute to the mountain and a promise that we will return someday, and started on our descent. We had a pleasant descent chatting with one or the other person and in a few hours we were down at the road.

My new friends invited me to have lunch with them and we had a nice meal at a little dhaba and then bid goodbye to them as they piled in their car and set out for the next trek. Ah- the joy of travelling alone... you can meet and mix with new people easily. One tends to stick to each other in a group.

I looked up nervously at the sky. It had clouded up and looked all ready to bucket down.

And just then my eye fell on the signboard of a hotel. Ah, wonderful! Let's stay here only - anyway, I was quite tired from the trek and didn't want to risk getting cramps while riding the bike. I got a nice ground floor room at a reasonable cost - and just as I brought my bike up and moved in...the heavens opened and it started pouring down!

Aha! Another perfect timing decision!

Thank you, Patron saint!

I got some hot water for a refreshing bath - and then just chilled in bed reading a book till dinner time.

* * *

Ah - What a wonderful day it had been!

Everything had been wonderful... the ride, the jungle, the trek, the views, the emotional storm at the temple, the chance meeting with new people, finding this lovely place to stay in...

Jai Baba Tungnath!

He had called, and I had come.

Deoriatal

I got up in the morning to the sound of pounding rain!

Oh no...it had not cleared up overnight after all - it was still raining and the electricity was still off. Oh well - at least the tea stall was working. I got myself a cup of tea and sat outside enjoying the sound of the rain and the whipping breeze.

Rain is so pleasant - as long as you don't have to be out in it.

I waited and tarried, waiting for the rain to stop - I had a bath, and breakfast, and another cup of tea… but alas, the rain continued unabated. Ah well…no point in sitting about waiting forever. If you have to ride in the rain, then you have to ride in the rain.

At least I had some decent rain gear this time - I had taken to wearing a Decathlon rain wear on top of my riding gear. This was a really nice product and kept out the rain pretty well - and kept you pretty comfortable. The best part was that the riding jacket and pants also remained dry and comfortable - and free from mud!

The weak point is always the gloves - however much the glove maker may swear that their gloves are totally waterproof - they never are. And being exposed to the wind and rain, they get soaked and waterlogged and by the end of the day your fingers end up looking like raisins.

But that was just too bad. Needs must, as the saying goes.

I geared and saddled up and kicked my bike to life and it roared to happy life! She was not afraid of the rain or slippery mountain roads! Bring it on, baby! ROAR!

I had thought of doing another trek today, to the high lake of Deoriyatal. WOOHOO! My third trek of the trip. But now I decided to skip it as it was cold and wet. I was looking towards the end of the trip now and didn't want to get stuck in the inevitable landslides and road closures that would be the result of so much rainfall.

Sorry Deoriyatal! I said - and immediately heard a derisive HAHAHA in my head.

What was that? I said, whipping my head about.

NOTHING. A voice in my head said. NOTHING AT ALL. HAHAHA.

I looked about and shrugged my shoulders.

Riding in the rains has its own charm - and riding in the rains in the mountains is especially amazing. The rain drops hit your helmet visor with a crisp pitter-patter and convert the whole view into an impressionist painting. The greens and browns and earth shades of the mountains mix with the broad shining black strip of the road and give you a feeling that you are high on the finest hash. The wind whooshes and screams in your ears and mixes with the steady thump-thump-pocketa-pocketa-thump-thump of the engine and it is as soothing as a bunch of Buddhist monks doing throat singing. The roads are sinuous and twisty and shiny like a snake shining in the sun, and you have to ride slow in the rain for safety's sake - so you can see the scenery as you ride. The scenery has been converted into an ever-changing impressionist landscape due to water flowing over the visor and you get a feeling of how Manet and Monet and Picasso must perceived the world around them.

You can feel your fingers getting wet and frozen and your right knee can feel the heat from the exhaust bent-pipe. Your warm breath causes your visor to fog up from the inside and you have to stop frequently to stop and wipe it off - but that is an excellent excuse to stop and look at the scenery.

I passed Makku village, which is where the priests of Tungnath hail from - and I smirk a bit, as Makku is the nickname of one of my close friends. I think of ringing him and congratulating him on having a whole village named after him - and maybe he should also audition to be the priest at Tungnath.

Just after Makku, I notice the turnoff for Sari village, which is the base of the Deoriyatal trek. I look at it some regret. All good things come in threes, they say… and I would have liked to do my third trek of the trip. But alas…sorry Deoriyatal.

HAHAHA

Eh? I looked around again - but there was no one in sight. I shrugged and rode on - and screeched to a halt!

Oh no! The road was blocked! Landslide!

I stood there and looked at it. The landslide must have just happened! Rocks and mud were still falling down. And I was the first vehicle there.

Shit. If I had been here just 5 minutes before, then I might have crossed it!

* * *

Oh well… if I had been here 4 minutes ago, it might have fallen on my head!

All that happens, happens for the best.

As I stood there, other vehicles came behind me and came to a halt and people came out to stare at the rockfall. Some were impatient - but most were philosophical about it. This was just another part of life, the way that traffic jams are part of life in Mumbai. No point railing against it.

The problem was that since the rockfall had literally just happened, it would take quite some to get cleared. Someone would have to go and tell the road-clearing team about it, then they would trundle up with their big earthmoving equipment and that might take some time. And anyway, they would have to wait for the landslide to stop completely - small rocks and mud was still falling continuously, and they would not want to risk getting stuck in another fall.

Hmm.

Some guys started turning around and going back. I was puzzled…where were they going? As far as I could see in my map, the only way around would be to go all the way back to Chamoli Gopeshwar and catch the highway there - which would be a really long diversion. Then someone told me that there was another road from Makku village. Really? I looked in my map - but there was no sign of any road.

'It's not on the map' one guy said 'But there is a road!'

Hmm… that sounded most suspicious. Either this guy was talking through his hat - or the road would be some insanely screwed little road. I had experience of these routes a number of times - the Pangi village route was still green in my memory! That route was so high and small and difficult that I was sure that I was going to take a high-dive in the river gorge on a number of occasions. (See 'Three Men Ride Again')

But after waiting for some time with no action, I got impatient. What was the point of waiting here? Might as well go to Makku and see if that road did indeed exist. If nothing else, it would be an adventure!

I turned my bike around and rode back and passed the turn-off to Sari village.

And I suddenly screeched to a halt!

Ah! Now I get it! This was a sign for me to go to Deoriyatal! Thats why the road was blocked!

HAHAHAHA…. I heard that amused laugh again…AT LAST HE GETS IT…

Oh all right - I am coming, I am coming. Don't get all upset.

I went up a most scenic and twisty road to Sari village, and found the path to Deoriyatal - a most unobtrusive little arch. I parked my bike in front of a dhaba and asked the proprietor if he would watch over my bike.

'We are always ready to help our customers.' He informed me with a deadpan face, and I laughed and ordered a cup of tea and a cream roll.

* * *

There were a bunch of trekkers there who seemed to have just come down from the trek, and asked them how it was.

'It's not too bad...' they assured me. 'The only problem was that it was raining...' he peered up at the sky. '... It seems to have cleared up now, though...'

Eh? I looked up and saw patches of blue sky! It had indeed stopped raining! Deoriyatal was welcoming me!

HAHAHAHA... again that laugh - but this time it was warm and encouraging.

I started climbing up that slope, using my usual tortoise technique...y'know...walk 500 mars, stop and catch breath... walk 500 mts...stop and catch breath...and repeat. On infinite loop. Every step takes you closer to your goal, after all.

I climbed up huffing and puffing, and suddenly I came upon a school! I was dumbstruck! Why have a school so high up above the village? But then, I suppose they were on the look out for any flat stretch of land, and this was the only one which was available and free. And probably students came from villages which were above and below the place - so it all evened out. And anyway, this much climb was a mere bagatelle for the hardy mountain folk...it was only fat plains-people who found it tough going!

The path became even more beautiful after that! And the advantage of my slow tortoise-step was that I had a lot of time to appreciate that wonderful greenery. What a lovely sight it was!

'A tiny guardian temple dedicated to the god Ganesh

spurred us on. Nor was I really fatigued for the cold fresh air and the verdant greenery surrounding us was like an intoxicant. Myriads of wild flowers grew on the hill slopes—buttercups, anemones, wild strawberries, forget-me-nots, rock-cress—enough to rival the Valley of Flowers at this time of the year.

Before reaching these alpine meadows, we climb through rhododendron forest and here one finds at least three species of this flower: the red flowering-tree rhododendron (found throughout the Himalayas between 6000 feet and 10,000 feet); a second variety, the almatta, with flowers that are light red or rosy in colour; and the third, chimul, or white variety, found at heights ranging from between 10,000 feet and 13,000 feet. The chimul is brushwood, seldom more than twelve feet high and growing slantingly due to the heavy burden of snow it has to carry for almost six months in the year.'

- Ruskin Bond

I also chanced upon a beautiful old temple! It was a classically built old temple, built in stone - and it looked lovely on that mountainside, though its look was a bit marred by an ugly metal sheet which someone had erected to get shelter from the rain. I went inside to take a look and get blessings for the trail.

I continued climbing - and finally I emerged on top!

WOOHOO! I was at Deoriyatal!

What a lovely place!

This lake, cradled on the hill at a height of 8,000 feet, was a favourite spot of one of Garhwal's earliest British Commissioners, J.H. Batten, whose administration continued for twenty years (1836-56). He wrote:

'The day I reached there, it was snowing and young trees were laid prostrate under the weight of snow; the lake was frozen over to a depth of about two inches. There was no human habitation, and the place looked a veritable wilderness. The next morning when the sun appeared, the Chaukhamba and many other peaks extending as far as Kedarnath seemed covered with a new quilt of snow, as if close at hand. The whole scene was so exquisite that one could not tire of gazing at it for hours. I think a person who has a subdued settled despair in his mind would all of a sudden feel a kind of bounding and exalting cheerfulness which will be imparted to his frame by the atmosphere of Duiri Tal.'

Alas for me - I couldn't get that wonderful sigh of Chaukhamba and the other peaks, as the whole sky was overcast. In clear weather the entire mountain range is reflected in that lake and looks magical - but I had no such luck.

But it was a lovely place to be nonetheless, and my soul rejoiced to see the place. The government has put a chowkidar there and there was a board saying that you had to pay a fee to enter the lake area. But the chowkidar was busily engaged with a pressure cooker trying to cook his lunch and was not interested in collecting any fees.

There was a punjabi dude there who was incandescent with rage that the government was demanding a fee! How dare they?
'But he is not asking for any fee.' I tried to console him.
'That is not the point! How dare they levy a fee?!'
Poor guy - he was so angry at the fee, that he was not able to enjoy the view at all. I left him fuming there and went off to explore the mountain top and that amazing lake on top of it.

* * *

I walked all around the lake revelling in the lovely misty cloudy atmosphere and marvelling at the varieties of trees and plants and shrubs - and the sight of various birds fluttering here and there. I found a secluded place with a lovely view of the surrounding countryside and sat there for some time meditating on the lovely views. One couldn't see the lofty Himalayan peaks - but the humble tilled fields and rolling forests below were also an enchanting sight.

I had to tear myself away finally and start on my downward walk. It was lunchtime already, and I would be hungry by the time I got down - and hopefully my dhabawala would not have gone off for a nap or something! It would be great to camp out here sometime…but since I had neither tent nor supplies, it was time to go back down.

I made my way down finally and went back to my friendly dhabawala, who was thankfully awake! I had a nice hot meal - and it turned out that the proprietor was an ex-mountaineer and used to be a coach at NIM - the Nehru Institute of Mountaineering! He was retired now, but still took groups of trekkers up the mountains.

A guy came over in a Maruti 800 … I thought he was a customer, but it turned out that he was the local newspaper distributor! The car was full of newspapers.

'But how will you complete your round?' I asked him. 'The road is closed due to landslide.'

'No no…it's open now.' He told me.

Well, that was good news!

I followed the Maruti car to the landslide point, and found that the road wasn't cleared after all. But a huge digger was making progress, and the path was cleared in 15-20 minutes -

and I went thankfully past that point.

Thankfully? Not entirely. A bit sadly, actually. My tryst with the high Garhwal was over. Now my path lay downwards! So sad!

I came down by the narrow winding roads to Ukhimath and passed Guptakashi - the 'Hidden Kashi' - where the holy rivers of Ganga and Yamuna were said to meet in secret at an underground spot, and there is a temple of Shiva as 'Vishwanath' here, just as it is in Varanasi. It is also part of the that load of Bull - where Shiva in the form of a bull disappeared into the ground and later the various dismembered parts reappeared in the places where the Panch Kedars are now.

I was a bit sick of the narrow twisty roads now - these roads are strong medicine, and should be taken in moderation! I was looking forward to hitting the main highway - 'Once I hit the main road, I will really twist that accelerator and zoom!' I thought.

But Alas! The main road was a disaster area, due to all the mountain cutting to expand the road. The road was a sea of slippery treacherous mud and streams of water, and the truck drivers seemed to take a lot of pleasure in liberally splattering me with mud as they zoomed by. Thank god for my rain gear.

I cursed and muttered as I grimly battled my way through that construction debris zone, and heaved a sigh of relief when I finally cleared it and came to a nice two-lane road. Thank god! I did not relish the idea of riding in that muddy, slippery and rather dangerous road in the dark!

I passed the town of Agastmuni - named after one of the

most revered sages in mythology - Rishi Agastya. In some scriptures, it is stated that during Lord Shiva's marriage, everyone in the universe went to witness the event in the Himalayas, in the North. Bhūmi Devi or the Earth Goddess was not able to bear this misbalance and prayed to Lord Shiva for help, who then told Agastya to go to the south end of India. Rishi Agastya went to the south and the earth's balance was restored. On one side there was the entire universe and on the other side was Agastya, whose austerity power and aura balanced the earth! In fact, he is also the reason why the Himalayas are the highest mountains in India! When he was crossing to the South, his way was barred by the mighty Vindhya mountains - which were as tall as the Himalayas at the time.

The Vindhya mountain was very happy when the revered sage Agastya came to it, and greeted him warmly, and Agastya blessed him. 'I need to go to the South as commanded by Lord Shiva - But how can I cross you?' Agastya asked him. 'You are so high and powerful'. And out of reverence for the sage, the mountain immediately bowed down and prostrated and became low and easy to cross.

'Please do remain like this till I come back.' Agastya said.

'Sure thing! Will do!' the Vindhyas promised - but Agastya never came back!

He remained permanently in South India and the Vindhyas are still low and prostrated, awaiting his return. And so the Himalayas became the highest mountains in India.

Because of this, Agastya rishi is most highly revered in South India! He is considered as the father of the Tamil language and compiler of the first Tamil grammar. There is a very large Agastya muni ashram in the South even today - which is famous now for being the source of 'Nadi Jyotish', a unique form of fortune telling. (See 'One Man Gets the Sack' for a fascinating history of Nadi Jyotish)

The town of Agastmuni blessed me as well! With a bottle of rum! I wanted to toast the successful treks and relax after what had been a fairly active and adventurous few days...but I just couldn't find a wineshop anywhere. Finally I stopped and asked a guy on the street if he knew where a wineshop was.

'Yes yes, of course!' he was absolutely enthusiastic, and actually walked me to the wineshop, which was almost hidden inside what looked like an underground bunker, where I scored a bottle of rum. What a nice fellow!

Now that I was well equipped, I kept a lookout for a nice hotel. I duly found a very nice place overlooking the river and settled in for the night - and toasted the trip with a dram of rum!

My high Garhwal adventure was over... now the road lay downhill...

Tehri - and back to Dehradun

Last night I had decided that I was done with the hard riding. I would take this beautiful two-lane expressway down to Rishikesh, find a nice backpacker joint by the river, and chill there - hopefully with some herbal application! Then maybe I will send the bike back from Haridwar station and take a cab to the airport.

But when I got up, I rebelled at this tame end to a glorious ride! The ride was ending - and I could not end it on such a dull note. 'Rage, rage against the dying of the light' and all that. I must explore as much as I can on this glorious last day.

I called up Bharathi -SHE WHO MUST BE OBEYED - and told her that I would be following her advice and going to Tehri and Musoorie and Dehradun after all.
'YOU MEAN YOU WERE ACTUALLY CONTEMPLATING

OF DISOBEYING MY ORDERS?' she roared disbelievingly - and I bit my tongue!

'No…no…not at all…her…heh…What I meant was …that as per your orders I will be going to Tehri and Dhanaulti and Mussoorie!'

'YOU BETTER! PUNY HUMAN! AAARGGHH! HULK SMASH!'

I duly packed up - and I noticed that the weather was packing up as well! It was cloudy and ominous and looked ready to soak me as soon as I set bum on bike.

Oh well.. It was the last day…let it pour. 'Blow, wind - and crack your cheeks' and all that. Wont matter if the gear gets wet and clammy now.

I had already paid the guy off last night, so I hopped on the bike and set out early. I would have breakfast on the road somewhere.

The highway ride was not very pleasant due to heavy traffic and all, and I was happy to see the turnoff to Tehri where I could get off the highway. The food and dhaba situation on small roads is not to be depended on, so I stopped at a likely-looking dhaba and had the inevitable aalu paratha breakfast - and was delighted to get an absolutely delicious piping-hot paratha! Aha! Yum! When the cook is uninspired and incompetent, you get a flat doughy tasteless thing which sits discontentedly in your tummy and complains at you - but when it is made by the right hands, it becomes a thing of joy!

As soon as I left the main highway, the road became extremely pleasant! Green and soothing, low traffic , pleasant rolling hills and a joy to ride on. I was really happy that I had not decided to take that highway to Rishikesh. I was riding beside a river - no doubt one of the many tributaries of the Ganga…every river here has to merge into the Ganga. The clouds had not lifted fully and there were patches of cloud still sitting on top of the river. It looked like the river was smoking!

'Smo-oke on the wa-ter … fire in the sky ay ay…' I sang loudly and my voice resonated inside my helmet, making me feel like a rock star! I love to sing - only I can't remember the words and I can't remember the tune, and cannot hold the tune even if I remember it. Strong men wince and run for cover when I sing, and I am summarily banned from parties and public events. Cows go off their milk and hens stop laying eggs and idli batter refuses to ferment.

Thus the only place I can sing in peace is when I am alone on my bike - and wearing my helmet!

'Sometimes I feel like singing. But I'm an out-of-tune singer; I can never hit the right note. People who are near me don't like to hear me singing, because odd things happen. If I'm in a car, singing, it goes off the road. Birds fall silent. Cows and other animals make a dash for safety. Schoolteachers go into shock. People do everything they can to prevent me from singing.'
- Ruskin Bond

Now it looked like my bike was complaining too! As soon as I started singing, the bike began coughing and groaning and throwing fits! The gears refused to engage and the chain restarted its ominous noises!

Oh shit! I really didn't want anything to happen out here in the middle of nowhere and with my flight the next day.

* * *

'OK OK…SORRY SORRY …' I yelled contritely, and patted my bike on the tank. 'Don't get so angry… I won't sing anymore.'

I proceeded on my rainy ride over the bee-yoo-tee-fool mountains and came to a delighted halt as I reached the top of a ridge and caught sight of a large lake!

I had reached Tehri dam! WOO HOO!

What a sight!

The Tehri dam was an awesome spectacle - a giant achievement of man over nature!

It's the highest dam in India and one of the highest in the world. They have built a 855 ft high mud and earth wall across the Bhagirathi river, and they have created a humongous 50 square km lake of a reservoir. Just think of it! 50 square kilometres! It holds a mind boggling 4 cubic kilometres of water! Thats 3.2 million acre-foot volume!

To put that in perspective - An acre-foot equals approximately an eight-lane swimming pool, 25 m long, 16 m wide and 3 m deep. That's 3.2 million of these pools right there!

This project is designed to produce 1000 MW of power and provide water for drinking and irrigation to all of North India. It is one of the longest running projects in the world - the first study took place in 1961 - and construction finally began in 1978 - and was finally operational in 2006!

This is also unfortunately one of the most bitterly contested environmental battles of India. Chipko movement leader and eco-warrior Sunderlal Bahuguna tried to fight it for over 20 years, saying that this is an environmental disaster and a death knell for the mountains and the local people! This giant dam is built in an extremely eco-sensitive zone and in one of the most high-earthquake risk areas of India and will drown untold acres of rich farmland - not to mention the entire town of Tehri!

Why do you want to build these humongous dams? He kept saying. These are a recipe for disaster! Build a series of small dams! Local people protested for years and years, and filed numerous court cases and did strikes and hartals and public protests.

But the Central Government - many governments over the years, various parties, various ideologies - all said 'Fuck you'!

We need the water and electricity, they said - and not to

mention the humongous bribes and kickbacks from the 1 Billion dollar cost of the dam. And we don't live there anyway - so why would we care about whether it screws up the ecology or not? Get lost! Get out of the way of progress - or we will shoot you down like dogs!

In fact, the local people started protesting when the first stage of dam building started - for a 600 MW project. Then the Soviet Union broke up and stopped bankrolling it - and then they thought that this might hold things up. But rather than holding things up - the government actually increased the project size to 1000 MW, and added two more dams for good measure - which will drown more than a 100 villages in the reservoir! Screw you locals! BUHAHAHA!

This issue of giant dams in India is fast reaching crisis proportions - and the issue is so confused now, that it is very difficult to know what is the correct way to proceed. The country definitely needs electricity and dependable water supply for its progress - but is environmental disaster worth it? We are already seeing giant floods every year - and the mega damage of the 2013 Uttaranchal floods is still green - or should be still green - in everyone's memory.

India has 4,857 large dams (more than 15 m in height or 10-15 m if it fulfils some other conditions) in operation and 314 under construction. While nine out of 10 dams in India have irrigation as their main purpose, in the Himalayan region, which accounts for 70 per cent of hydel power potential - it is mostly for power generation. India, China, Nepal and Bhutan are in a race to build dams for hydro power.

As all these rivers are meltwater rivers, climate change will definitely mess up the dam planning severely if the glaciers melt off, or rains become undependable - and where will we be then?

I rode slowly down the road admiring the titanic scale of the dam, and got an awesome view of the dam wall from the height. It was simply enormous! 66 feet wide at the crest! There was a blacktop road running right on top of it!

I would love to take a joy ride on this! But will they allow me?

I went down to the dam wall and asked the CISF guy whether I could be allowed to go for a joy ride on the dam wall.

He gave me a disbelieving look.

'Where do you want to go... what is your destination for the day?' he asked.

'Mussoorie' I said - wondering why he was asking my

destination when all I wanted was to ride on the wall for a bit.

'I can't allow you to take a joyride…' he said.

'Aww…' I said disappointedly

'…But you have to go on that road anyway! That is the road to Mussoorie!'

'Oh? Really?'

'Yes…so do ride across… but no stopping! And no photographs!'

'Oh great! Thanks!'

It was then that I noticed that a Uttarakhand roadways bus was driving across the dam! So much for being a forbidden site.

I rode slowly across the dam wall and noticed that the place was festooned with security cameras, and no doubt the stoppers and gawker and photo takers would be caught and fined as soon as they crossed the wall!

Once I was away from all the security hassle, I stopped at a roadside stall to get out of the rain and had a cup of tea and a bun.

While the actual dam wall is a high security zone, the backwaters of the dam are being promoted as a tourism attraction. The Government of Uttaranchal is promoting it as a nice destination for holidaymakers from Delhi and NCR and are promoting adventure activities like paragliding, jet skiing and banana boats, and also houseboats and water hut and that kind of stuff. And of course, just the sight of the dam and water flow is pretty cool to see as well.

They are even planning to sell the drowned old town as a tourist attraction. As per a newspaper report, the Uttaranchal government is planning to turn lost town of Tehri -- buried under Tehri dam -- into a tourist hotspot by using submarine-like vessels!

In 2017, Tourism minister Satpal Maharaj gave an interview to the Hindustan Times and said that the structures of old Tehri town were still intact and would offer a thrilling experience to tourists.

"Small submarines will be employed for underwater tourism. Watching an underwater township from a submarine that will have transparent body will be new experience for tourists. We hope to make it reality in coming days,"

The minister said structures like clock tower, Purana Darbar, Naya Darbar, Swami Ram Teerath Ashram, main market area, Pakoriwali Gali of the submerged town would be major tourist attractions.When implemented, the project would increase inflow of foreign tourists in the hill state, Maharaj said, adding that transparent body submarines were made specially for under water tourism activities. "These are already being used in several parts of the world particularly in Australia."

Now that's Chutzpah for you! Drown the feller - and then sell the corpse!

I left Tehri and its watery grave behind, and carried on towards Dhanaulti and Mussoorie. It was extremely beautiful ! But also rainy and windy and cold and I was slowly turning into a soggy icicle. It was fun and all - but after hours of fighting through cold and rain, your spark does tend to get extinguished.

When I studied that map, I realised that Landour is actually a suburb of Mussoorie - and Landour was where Ruskin Bond lived! Wow!

* * *

As you might have noticed by now, I am a big fan of Ruskin Bond - have been one since childhood. He is the true bard of Uttarakhand and his charming and evocative writing about the hills and people and stories of Dehradun and it's surroundings really touch a chord with me - as indeed with most Indian readers. I developed a great love for mountains, for childhood, for simple people and nature by reading his books. Whether its his fiction or auto-biographical works or his occasional poetry - I loved it all.

So I thought that this would be a great opportunity to ride into Landour and meet Ruskin Bond. I wouldn't go as far as to go and knock at his door and disturb his afternoon nap - he has cribbed about that many times in many books. In fact he dedicated one of his books thus -
    'In the spirit of goodwill, tolerance and ahimsa,
    I dedicate this book
    to all those who come knocking at my door
    in the middle of my afternoon siesta.
    May they too discover the benefits
    and pleasures of a good afternoon's sleep.'

Well - I completely empathise… I love my afternoon nap myself and that seems to be the time when all the telephone spammers call me and offer me credit cards and timeshare holidays and insurance and stuff. I wouldn't want to end up as a villain in a future book, so I would not actually go and knock at his door and disturb his siesta - but I had heard that he drops into his favourite bookshop in Landour now and then, and signs autographs for fans - much to the bookseller's delight I am sure, because the fans would have to buy a book first.
* * *

WOOHOO! I AM GOING TO MEET RUSKIN BOND! I thought.

But even the thought of meeting a literary hero couldn't keep me warm in that continuous rain and finally after coming through a particularly windy pass where the wind cut through my jacket with a scornful laugh - I could stand it no more and was most happy to see a hotel! I stopped there and went shivering into that hotel slavering for hot tea and a bite to eat.

'BRRR' I said to said to the hotelier. 'C-C-Can I have some eggs?'
But the guy shook his head. No eggs here. Shoo.
Eh? Why not?
Because of the temple, of course.
Temple? What temple?

It turned out that I had stopped - entirely without intending to - at the base of the Surkanda Devi temple.

Wow! Another diety summoning me!

Surkanda Devi, as I later learnt, is a 'shaktipeetha' - which is part of a fairly gruesome legend.

When Sati, the daughter of the great demi-god Daksha insisted on marrying Lord Shiva - Daksha was not happy with Sati's choice and did not consider the ash-smeared, half-naked, mountain-dwelling, ganja-smoking Shiva to be a suitable son-in-law for himself.
One day Daksha threw a grand party and invited the whole world for his shindig - but pointedly did not invite Shiva or even his own daughter Sati. Sati was eager to attend the party

and thought that her invitation must have got lost in the mail or something and so turned up at the party anyway - eager to see dear old Dad and all her friends.

To her shock, dear old Dad cut her dead- and probably sniffed about deadbeats and panhandlers and people who come uninvited to parties and so on, and jeered at her and her husband.

Sati was so shocked and angry...that she committed suicide! There and then! She called on the fires of heaven to burn her alive! Right in the middle of the party! Talk about an over-reaction! I mean...a normal person would have given her dad a nasty look or thrown some utensils around - but to set yourself on fire...ew!

Daksha must have had a nasty shock - but carried on with the party nevertheless.

Unfortunately for him, Shiva was the most powerful of all gods - and when he got pissed, he really lost it! He went crazy when he heard the news (understandably) and sent a fearsome demon to crash the party and kill everyone there! (Maybe a little over the top there - but he became a hero to all husbands who disliked their father's in law)

After that explosion of rage, Shiva was lost in grief and carried the body of the dead Sati in his arms and travelled all over the universe - casting a downer on every living thing. People sympathised for some time, but then got sick of it... but they were understandably afraid to mention it to Shiva...he had just killed everyone at the party after all, and had threatened to destroy the universe by performing the Tandava dance! So they went to Vishnu and begged him to do something about it. Vishnu decided to remove the locus of his sadness and despair by disposing of the body of Sati.

* * *

So - here's the gory part - he sent his divine discus, the 'Sudarshan chakra' to act as a sort of flying circular saw, and gradually chopped the body of Sati into pieces! Bits of her fell here and there, and the places they fell became sacred and were worshipped as 'shakti peetha' or 'place of power'. After some time Shiva had no body in his arms and so he gradually forgot his grief and came back to normalcy. Out of sight, out of mind.

There are 51 shakti peethas all over sub-continent - distributed over what is now India, Pakistan, Sri Lanka, Nepal, Bangladesh and Tibet (China). This shows that Vishnu did a real number on that body! Chopped it to bits! You have temples dedicated to weird parts like lips, throat, portion between the eyebrows, navel, eyes…and the most powerful one is where her vagina fell - in Kamakhya, near Guwahati, Assam.

* * *

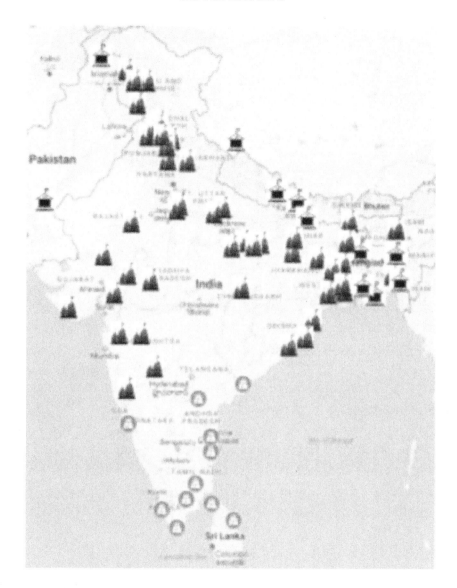

This place was apparently where her head fell (assumably what was left of the head - after lips, ears, eyes, eyebrows, place between brow and so on were removed and fell in other places). Thus the place was called 'Sir khand' or 'place where head fell', which was later corrupted to 'Surkanda'.

* * *

Where is the temple? I asked - since I was not getting eggs anyway, I might as well take advantage of my eggless purity to go and meet Surkanda Devi and pay my respects.

Right up there - the hotelwala said - pointing his finger straight up!
Eh?
I went and looked outside, and the mist lifted to show the start of a staircase. I looked up …and up…and up…and had to really crane my neck to see the temple on a lofty perch.

Shit. This temple was very high up! What a climb!

And just as I was looking, the mist came down again and a nasty wind blew right through me and naughtily deposited a few raindrops down my collar!

EEEEK! I squealed and scuttled indoors and leaned over the cooking stove to warm myself.

I was too cold and wet and tired to be climbing so many steps, I said - and decided not to visit the temple, and did an obeisance to Surkanda Devi from the hotel itself and left after my chai and snacks.

I had to rush if I wanted to meet Ruskin Bond!

And I could just feel a disapproving eye on the back of my neck and a voice saying 'NO TIME TO SEE ME, EH? WE SHALL SEE…WE SHALL SEE…'

'What was that?' I asked, looking around wildly - but all I heard was a disapproving sniff.

* * *

I carried on from Dhanolti and came within a stone's throw to Mussoorie. I was just congratulating myself on having completed the trip successfully and was already fantasising about meeting Mr Bond and was composing opening line to say to him - 'Hello Mr Bond'… 'Whassaap Rusk?' … 'Hi Rusty!' … 'ooooh oooooh ooooh… I am a huge fan….ooooh oooh' … 'hello 007 - may I see your license to thrill?'

I was just trying them all out and wondering which one would thrill Ruskin bond so much that he would jump up from his seat and say 'This is the fan I was looking for all my life! What wit! What erudition! What delivery! What style!' and maybe he would embrace me and kiss me on both cheeks… MUAH MUAH..

Hmmm

Maybe not the kiss bit… edit that out…

Hmmm

Maybe not the embrace either….cut that too…

Hmmmm

CLONK CLONK CLONK CLONK

A most nasty noise hastily brought me out of my pleasant

mediations and my bike started to make the most alarming sounds and lost power completely!

AAARGGH.. . I weaved a bit and then got the bike under control and came to a halt.

WHAT THE HELL WAS THAT?

I parked the bike and put it on the main stand - and saw to my utter shock that the bloody chain had come off! It had come off the rear wheel and was hanging limply!

I couldn't believe my eyes!

I had never seen anything like this before in all my riding. What was this? A bloody bicycle? I looked disbelievingly at that huge chain hanging down. How had this even happened?

And what was I supposed to do about it? I slowly took out my took kit and slowly and laboriously put the chain back on the sprocket with the aid of a pair of screwdrivers - but I looked at it most doubtfully. If the chain had gone back on so easily, then it would come off again just as easily!

Shit shit shit.

I looked at the rolling hills and realised that this was no place for a breakdown of any sort… there was no civilisation around, and no repair shops and no way to push the giant Enfield up the slope!

Crossing my fingers, my toes and eyes - I started the bike again and was much relieved when the engine roared and the bike started moving. But it was a short lived joy as the bloody chain came off again after some time. Cursing freely, I again put the bike on stand and got to work with the screwdriver.

But I am utterly useless with any kind of tool and this time I was not able to get the chain back on. I looked at my grease stained palms ruefully and was wondering what to do, when again heard that mocking laughter.

HAHAHAHAHA....

NO TIME TO SEE ME EH?

WANTED TO SEE RUSKIN BOND, EH?

HAHAHAHAHAHA

Oh no! It was Surkanda Devi!

'I am sorry!' I wailed. 'I am so so so sorry! I won't do it again! I promise!'

Whether it was the goddess getting appeased by my remorse, or the arresting sight of a fat grease-stained biker talking to himself - a biker came and stopped in front of me! It was like a gift from god!

'Having trouble?' he asked

'YES!' I shouted, and subsided as I saw the guy jerk back in alarm. 'Er... I mean...yes, yes...the bloody chain is coming off.'

That nice fellow got off his bike and got on his knees and did all the heavy work of putting the chain back on, while I just stood by and chilled and whistled. He was clearly sent by my protector - the Patron Saint of Idiots.

'Well...that's back on...' he said finally, all grease and mud stained - 'You are back in action.'

* * *

'Hey thanks a ton!' I said 'lets hope it stays fixed.'

I thanked him brokenly and he just smiled and waved it off, and got on his bike and rode off. I packed up my tools again, and put the saddlebags back on and again started the bike. I started riding very slowly so as to stress that chain as little as possible.

I made it almost to the top of the hill - I was literally within 10 metres of it - when the chain came off for the third time! Oh no! I got off the bike and pushed it up the hill - and just pushing it those 10 meters was enough to wipe me out!

OOF. PUFF. GASP.

What to do now? I saw that there was a restaurant at the top of the hill and there were a lot of bikes parked outside it. Chalo, might as well have a cup of tea and ponder over the situation. Things are always better after a cup of tea.

'Arre! You again? What happened?'
I looked up - to see the face of my good samaritan friend, who had helped me earlier. He was a part of that group of bikers who had stopped at the restaurant.

'That damn chain came off again.' I told him pathetically. 'I had to push the bike here.'
'Ah yes… you need a mechanic.' He told me.
'Yes…but there is no one around…' I said.
'Don't worry sir, and have a cup of tea.' He said. 'We will help you.'

* * *

And that incredibly good fellow rode all the way down to Mussoorie - found a mechanic - made the guy leave his shop - and brought him all the way to where I was!

And I was relaxing with a cup of tea!

Incredible!

Fantastic!

What good fellows! They were all working in a branch of the Oriental Bank in Saharanpur, and had come out for a weekend bike ride. They had absolutely no obligation to help me - but they not only went out of their way to go and get that mechanic for me, but didn't even allow me to pay for my tea! They just brushed off my thanks with a smile, and rode off.

I was left in a warm glow of thankfulness.

Thank you, kind gentlemen from Oriental bank, Saharanpur! May you have all happiness in life!
Thank you mechanic, for leaving your shop and coming!
Thank you India for having such lovely helpful people everywhere!
Thank you Patron Saint of Idiots for consistently bailing me out of sticky spots!

AHEM

Ah yes... Thank you Surkanda Devi, for forgiving me!

IGNORE ME FOR RUSKIN BOND, WILL YOU?
* * *

No no no no no…. I stammered. Never! I will not even look in his direction! I will pass him by! I will not even get off my bike in Landour! He can remain in the room on the roof for all I care! Let him remain a vagrant in the valley! If I see the Cambridge book depot in Landour bazaar, I shall shudder and look away like Lot looking away from Sodom and Gomorrah! Even if I see him on the road, I shall put my nose up and walk away snootily!

HAHAHAHAHA

The mechanic finished his mystic passes over my bike and hey presto! It was working again! I had all the awe for him that a little child has for a magician who has made a coin appear from his ear.

I dropped the mechanic back to his shop, and he charged me a very modest amount for his labours.

'Better get that chain and sprocket changed when you get back to Bombay.' He told me. 'I have tightened the chain, but that's only a stopgap measure.'

I again cursed the Royal Enfield team of the Tour of Uttarakhand - but hey, all it needed to do now was to survive a few kilometres more. I could almost see Dehradun from here.

My route did indeed take me through Landour Bazaar - and I was rather stunned to see a long line of book lovers standing outside that book shop. Mr Bond was going to have a cramp in his palm from signing so many books!

A pity I had made that promise - but to be honest, I was only concerned with getting back to Dehradun now! The chain was creaking again, and now the brakes were making alarming noises and the gear was gnashing and refusing to engage every now and then. Looks like the Devi still had her eye on me!

I am going, I am going - I assured her, and went right past the bookshop and all the way down to Doon. It was an extremely steep slope, and I was in mortal fear till I came down to the town - the bloody brake should not be the thing to give way now!

I found a nice hotel using a hotel booking app and gratefully crawled into a nice room and moaned with pleasure as I took off my wet clothes and took a hot bath.

Aaaah! Hot bath at close of day!

Sing hey! for the bath at close of day
That washes the weary mud away!

A loon is he that will not sing:
O! Water Hot is a noble thing!

O! Sweet is the sound of falling rain,
and the brook that leaps from hill to plain;
but better than rain or rippling streams
is Water Hot that smokes and steams.

O! Water cold we may pour at need
down a thirsty throat and be glad indeed;
but better is Beer if drink we lack,
and Water Hot poured down the back.

O! Water is fair that leaps on high
in a fountain white beneath the sky;
but never did fountain sound so sweet
as splashing Hot Water with my feet!

- Bilbo's bath song - Tolkein

Back home

I had gone to sleep with a very specific plan in mind - I would ride the bike down to the Dehradun railway station, despatch the bike by train parcel, then take all my luggage and get a taxi to the Dehradun airport and then take my direct flight back to Mumbai- the ticket for which had been booked a long time back.

And interestingly - none of these plans worked out!

First of all, I woke up to a lovely sight of overcast skies and cloudy valleys and the musical pitter-patter of rain on the windows. While rain was absolutely lovely to contemplate whilst I was comfortably indoor and dry and warm - I had no wish to venture out into the rain again. That full days soaking of yesterday had been quite enough, thank you.

I had my packet tea and continued to see the rain pour down, and became more and more reluctant to ride the bike in this rain. The bike's struggles of yesterday were painfully fresh in my mind, and the poor thing was clearly worn out and exhausted after 20 days in the mountains. It was in desperate need of TLC - and I did not relish the idea of the bike breaking down in the middle of Dehradun - in the middle of this rainstorm - while I rode down to the railway station.

Even after reaching the station, I would have to do all the jumping through hoops to register the bike as a parcel, drain the tank, get it packed and loaded and so on. And I would have to do the whole process in reverse in Mumbai - go to the railway station, claim the bike, fill petrol and ride it home or to the workshop…and hope like hell that it would not break down on the way!

Hmmmpff.

Finally I decided that it would be much simpler to send the bike by road courier - the courier guy would pick up the bike from the hotel in Dehradun and deliver it at my home in Mumbai. It would cost a little bit more, and would take a few days longer... but it would be pain-free. I called up the courier guys and negotiated costs and arranged for the guy to come and pick up the bike from the hotel. I packed all my wet riding gear and helmet on the bike so that I would be flying home with only a small hand bag.

The guy duly came and took away my bike in style in a smart little truck- like a girl going to her husbands place in a royal palanquin!

* * *

Ah! What a relief! The bike was safe and sound and would soon be in the warm embrace of my mechanic, who would restore it back to its growling glory

The next thing to do was to take a cab to the airport. I thought that it would be a most simple thing - just book an Uber and it would take you there.

The cab did come as per booking - but when he learnt of my destination…he refused to go!

'No no no no…. I can't take you to the airport sir…please get out of my cab and take another one!'

'Eh? Why?'

It turned out that the local taxi fellows have a racket going and do not allow Ola or Uber cabs to go to the airport - and threaten to beat them up if they do so!

'But where will I get a cab now?' I whined 'There is not much time left for the flight.'

Finally the guy agreed to take me there if I paid a slightly higher figure - and in cash - so that he could truthfully claim that he was not an Uber driver, but just a private taxi.

I was OK with that, and he happily drove me to the airport and even stopped at his favourite roadside dhaba for chai and snacks.

At the airport - there was another problem! The pouring rain had delayed all the flights! And there was pandemonium at the airport, with the worried airline people not knowing what to do.

I was booked on Jet Airways - and the Jet airways manager came to me and asked me if I was willing to go on Indigo airlines instead - via Delhi, instead of my direct flight to Mumbai.

'Eh? Why?'

'Sir.. I don't know if and when our flight will come - when will it finally come in and when it will leave... so I am trying to get my guests out as soon as possible.'

I looked at him narrowly - either he was an extremely-ordinarily good man (rare) or had overbooked his flight like crazy and was trying to shunt people to other flights.

Then I shrugged. Why should I not assume that he is a nice guy?

I choose to assume that he is a nice guy and is trying to do the right thing.

I agreed to go by the Indigo flight via Delhi - and as it ultimately turned out, the Jet direct flight from Dehradun, and the Indigo hopping flight from Delhi both landed in Mumbai within minutes of each other!

And that was it.

The ride was over - and I was back in Mumbai.

It was a shame I did not get to meet RB in Landour, but then I was off to meet my own RB at home (R Bharathi - SHE WHO MUST BE OBEYED) and so 'All's well that ends well'.

I was glad indeed to be home after 20+ days of riding in the mountains.

But already I was making plans to return!

I want to ride more in Uttarakhand! I want to go to Gangotri,

Yamnotri, Nilang valley - I want to trek, I want to go river rafting in the Ganga...

To quote RB one last time...

Once you have lived with mountains
Under the whispering pines
And deodars, near stars
And a brighter moon,
With wood smoke and mist
Sweet smell of grass, dew lines
On spider-spun, sun-kissed
Buttercup and vine;
Once you have lived with these,
Blessed, God's favourite then,
You will return,
You will come back
To touch the trees and grass
And climb once more the windswept mountain pass.

- Ruskin Bond

The end

Before you go…

Thank you so much for reading this book!

A request - Please do leave a REVIEW on Amazon - reviews are like oxygen for Self Published Authors, and we need all the help we can get! Do help out if you can - with star ratings, text reviews - even video reviews are possible.

And of course - do tell all your friends on Goodreads, Facebook, Twitter, Instagram etc.

Check out all PHOTOS of this trip at

www.ketanjoshi.net

OTHER INTERESTING STUFF YOU MAY LIKE - BLOG, YOUTUBE AND PODCAST

PODCAST - I have a **PODCAST** - **Travel with Ketan** - available on Anchor.fm, Spotify, Google Podcasts, Apple podcasts etc. I have been doing a reading of 'Three Men on Motorcycles - The Amigos ride to Ladakh' on that - so you can enjoy the book while walking, running, jogging, driving etc. If you like stories, but have no time or inclination to actually curl up with a book - then this option is best for you.

* * *

And I have a rocking **YOUTUBE Video channel** - **KetanWrites** - where I tell ride stories - with a bit of acting and fun, and illustrated with photos and videos. I have been doing a reading of my book 'Three Men Ride Again - The Amigos ride to Spiti', and its a blast! - go to my website. Try them out - they are a blast!

    BLOG And I have a blog - Ketan's Blog - where I write about various topics - smaller trips which I have not written books about, opinion pieces, new book announcements, interesting tidbits and news. It's great fun - l have posted a series of articles of my exploration of Mumbai by cycle. Do check it out on www.ketanjoshi.net/blog

WWW.KETANJOSHI.NET

you will find all **PHOTOS** of the ride there, my **BLOG**, my **PODCAST** and my **YOUTUBE** channel, **CONTACT ME** and all kinds of interesting stuff.

And of course - Do write to me on ketan@ketanjoshi.net . I would love to hear from you.

    Follow me on **Facebook, Twitter and Instagram- @ketanwrites**

Have you checked out my other books? All of them are great fun.

The Amigos series

Three Men on Motorcycles -   The Amigos Ride to Ladakh

Three Men Ride Again - The Amigos Ride to Spiti
Three Men Ride South- The Amigos Ride to Coorg
Three Men Ride the Cliffhanger- The Amigos Ride the Most
Dangerous Roads in the World
Three Men Ride West - The Amigos ride to Gujarat
and Diu

The Backpacking series

One Man Goes Backpacking - The Amigo @ Kumbh Mela
One Man Goes Trekking - With SHE WHO
MUST BE OBEYED to Everest Base Camp
One Man Goes on a Bus - With SHE WHO MUST BE
OBEYED Spiti and Leh by bus
One Man Gets the Sack - And travels the world
One Man Goes Cycling - Mumbai to Goa! Or Bust!

The Fiction collection

Bombay Thrillers - Thrilling short stories
Dipy Singh - Private detective. - Stories of a really fun
Indian detective, and me as his sidekick
Dipy Singh and the Mystery of the Office Rat - A novel.

Printed in Great Britain
by Amazon

78090730R00139